Seven Steps to wealth...

All the things they don't usually tell you about purchasing an investment property

2nd Edition

John L Fitzgerald

Seven Steps to Wealth

First published in Australia in 1998 by
Toogoolawa Children's Home Ltd.

Reprinted – 1998
Second edition: July 1999
© 1998 John L Fitzgerald

Every effort has been made to trace the copyright holders of statistical information and diagrams reproduced in this book. The author is grateful to BIS Shrapnel, The Real Estate Institute of Australia, Residex, Business Review Weekly, ANZ Bank and the Australian Bureau of Statistics for permission to use selected data.

No responsibility can be accepted by the author or publisher of this book for any action taken by any person or organisation relating to any material contained herein. Property investment is a complex and constantly changing field, and all readers should seek independent and detailed advice as to the relevance of any part of this material to their own specific circumstances.

National Library of Australia Cataloguing-in-Publication data
Fitzgerald, John L., 1963-
Seven Steps to Wealth: all the things
they don't usually tell you about purchasing an investment property.

Includes index.
ISBN 0 9585416 20

1. Real estate investment - Australia.
I. Toogoolawa Children's Home Ltd. II. Title
332.6320994

Text by John L Fitzgerald and Claire Louise Wright
First edition edited by Claire Louise Wright
Designed and typeset by Evolution Communications Pty. Ltd.
Illustrations by Dennis Holmes
Printed in Australia by Australian Print Group

Contents

To all custodians,

especially Deborah and Christine,
pillars of strength.

Preface

This is not just a book about how to build wealth by investing in real estate. It's a book about how *you* can build wealth by investing in real estate.

There's a big difference. The words 'property investment' probably conjure up visions of serious guys in serious suits talking about things like 'negative gearing' and 'leverage' and 'equity positions'. And for most people, that's a major turn-off. Perhaps that's why property investment is one of the best kept secrets of the financial world...

I'm going to let you into a *few* well-kept secrets in this book - and I'm going to try and do it in easy-speak language that anyone can pick up and read. I figure, if Steven Hawking can write a popular book based on Einstein's Theory of Relativity, then somebody ought to be able to do the same for real estate investment! I'd like to give you something you can relate to and, more importantly, use - without constantly tripping over a load of jargon and statistics.

The books on wealth creation that *are* full of jargon and statistics (and there are a few of them about) are often written by academics who may have gathered a wealth of theoretical knowledge - but haven't actually, personally, created any wealth. I'd have to say, I'm pretty much the opposite.

However, Einstein himself said: 'Everything should be made as simple as possible, but not any simpler.' Good rule. So you *will* find numbers and charts and technical terms in this book, but they are there to clarify key concepts - *not* to prove that I can use statistics and big words! We'll also cover a fair bit of information, but this isn't one of those 'everything you never particularly wanted to know about economics' books. I'm simply going to tell you about the most effective way I know to build wealth.

At the end of this book, you will have a pretty clear idea of how to maximise your assets, reduce your tax bill, ask the right questions - *and* see through some of the so-called experts in the field. And, perhaps most importantly, you'll know that *you can* build wealth.

The principles set out in this book aren't new. I've been using them for myself, and for clients, for over 10 years - and they work. They've given us financial freedom, security and a great lifestyle for ourselves and our families. And that's just one part of what building wealth is about. For me, it's also about the potential to make a difference in the world: an opportunity to be all I can be. I think of it as a journey to discover *purpose*.

Welcome to the adventure.

Foreword

to the Second Edition

A lot has happened since the first edition of *Seven Steps to Wealth*. The book took on a life of its own: redefining some boundaries for government legislation, banks, real estate marketers and their agents, developers and, most importantly, investors.

The purpose of the first edition was to outline to the 'average' investor how he or she could build wealth. That, in a nutshell, meant unveiling some misnomers and mistruths within the industry.

Since the first edition, we have been deluged with media stories exposing the marketers who are selling overpriced units in Sydney, Melbourne and especially on the Gold Coast, and who are charging outrageous commissions of $30,000 or $40,000. These marketers offer unrealistic capital growth projections and use all sorts of tricks, including telemarketing and high pressure lures, to get people along to their seminars.

The Minister for Fair Trading in Queensland put her hand up to try and change the legislation. She came out guns blazing and, (after flicking through a copy of *Seven Steps to Wealth*) decided that agents' disclosing their commissions and banks' disclosing their valuations would be a great way to go. The most recent report is that the Minister is going to settle for establishing a 'cooling off' period: the disclosure of bank valuations and commissions 'will be further reviewed'!

I laughed to see the banks squirm when tackled on the differential between a property's sale price and their bank valuation and, more importantly, on why they don't disclose their valuations. NAB and Westpac both came out and admitted that their valuations don't represent market value and advised purchasers to do their own investigation. I make the point strongly in Chapter 7: if you are going to build wealth in property, you must have a copy of the bank valuation and ensure that it reflects market value.

Why wouldn't it? Well, the bank's valuation may exclude fixtures and fittings, or not include the full total for landscaping and other items. It may be based on a quick or forced sale (within a 90-day period). It may be based on comparables sales in a completely different area.

The long and short of it is that banks look after themselves. You need to do the same if you want to invest in property.

For this second edition, I have updated all the graphs with the latest statistics and figures. The graphs are really there to suggest how and where you can source information. Chase specifics rather than statistics. In real estate, people quote statistics all the time, but tend to lose sight of the specifics.

Just an example, probably the greatest load of hogwash I have read in the last year (and keep on reading) is the pundits' quoting of the 'median house price' as the barometer of growth in real estate. Why isn't this right? Because real estate is *land:* not buildings. The fact is that, as we discuss in Chapter 4, land appreciates and buildings depreciate. And the average size of a block of land has been steadily shrinking, particularly within a 15-20km radius of the city. So when pundits talk about 'median house price over the last 10-20 years', they are referring to houses with allotments often double or triple the size of today's average. Not exactly comparing apples with apples. In fact, growth in the value of the *land* may have gone up by 400-500%, but that may not be reflected in the median house price.

So when you read an article or report referring to capital growth of property and quoting the median house price as a gauge, file it away in the bin, because that is where it belongs. The median house price can suggest a general trend over a 10-year period, but it doesn't get down to the specifics of actual capital growth and land content. This is the kind of information you need to search out yourself.

Once you start doing your own homework, I would recommend a visit to the Australia Bureau of Statistics' (ABS) on-line data. As an example, in Chapter 4 I talk about location as an important issue in where to invest and in Chapter 5, I note the average Australian household is still 2.8 persons. For us to build wealth as investors, we therefore need to identify suburbs that meet our location criteria with three or more persons per household. The ABS is a good source of such information. It can also give you specifics such as the income profile of an area, and the ratio of owner-occupiers to renters.

Finally, since the first edition of *Seven Steps to Wealth*, the GST has entered the final throes of legislation. I am often asked how that will impact on negative gearing. In truth, it won't have a major impact. Those on an income of $45,000 per annum receive just under 20% deduction in their PAYE tax, and those on incomes in excess of $50,000 a diminishing reduction.

What will be interesting in the final draft of legislation is whether and how the GST will differentiate between 'house price' and the cost of acquiring a block of land and building a home (see Chapter 6).

The main thing about building wealth is to focus on your goal. The many, many letters that I have received since the first edition of *Seven Steps to Wealth* have suggested that the book has given 'ordinary' Australians a new perspective and a new belief that they too can build wealth. There is no better feeling for me than when somebody who has read the book gives me that kind of feedback: thank you.

Let me leave you, for now, with an age-old saying. 'The past is history. The future is uncertain. But the present is a gift.' Use that gift to the best of your ability — for you, your family and your community. Be all you can be — Chapter 10.

John L Fitzgerald
June 1999

Introduction

A FOOL AND HIS MONEY
ARE EASILY PARTED

There are really only two reasons why you would lose money in real estate.

1 Greed.

2 Not doing your homework.

Unfortunately, those two things catch out about 95% of 'punters'.

Greedy investors are usually locked into Get Rich Quick thinking - and they shoot themselves in the foot in all sorts of ways: making false economies, pricing themselves out of the market, selling short of real growth. As an investor, unfortunately, you also need to avoid being manipulated by the greed of others - and there's a fair bit of it about in the real estate industry. That's why doing your homework is so important.

The real estate industry is huge: the residential sector alone turns over $22,327 million per year. That's a lot of property. And it's often bought and sold less on sound research and decision-making than on sentiment, impulse, gut feeling - and, of course, 'expert opinion'. (Multi-billion-dollar industries seem to attract 'expert opinions' in about equal quantities.)

I forever have people walk into my office saying they've bought *the* property that is going to make them a lot of money, or that they represent a vendor or particular property that I've just *got* to acquire if I want to make money. Over the years, I have learned not to get too excited: probably 1 in 100 of these people has any idea at all what he or she is talking about. It's a bit like McDonalds Restaurants: everyone thinks they can set up a duplicate fast food chain, because McDonalds make it look like such a simple business. It isn't - and thousands have failed in the attempt.

I'm reminded of this every year, on my pilgrimage to the AFL Grand Final. Everybody has a strong opinion about the game, before, during and after it's played! Our opinions don't always coincide, and - frankly - aren't always based on sober fact or objective analysis. And that's our right to free speech! Sitting among the spectators, you could well believe that the person next to you would make a *far* better umpire than the umpire - and certainly a better coach than the guys in the box. The fact is, however, that umpires and coaches have paid their dues in the little league, or with other football clubs, and then graduated through the majors: they are appointed on their track record, and judged on their track record, game by game, as their career goes on.

> **There are literally thousands of people giving advice about what to buy or sell, and quite a lot of them simply haven't got a clue!**

The real estate industry has all the opinions - and not too many of the track records to support them. There are literally thousands of people giving advice about what to buy or sell, and quite a lot of them simply haven't got a clue! Others, of course, have their own good reasons for giving bad advice. And if you take that advice: sorry, but you are probably a fool - and guess what will happen to you and your money...

It sometimes seems like there's a 'veil of mystery' (or perhaps it's just confusion) over property investment. If you're going to make good decisions that will build you wealth, you need to look behind two veils.

- Why are you buying a property? and
- Who is selling or advising you to buy it - and why?

There are really only three reasons to buy a property.

1   For your *own use:* that is, to live or work in.

2   For *income:* that is, to supplement your income in the short term, through charging rent, and taking advantage of legitimate tax deductions.

3   For *capital growth.* That's what builds wealth, and it is going to be the purpose we focus on throughout this book.

I travel all around Australia talking to people about building wealth in real estate. A lot of them have already acquired some sort of investment property, and when I ask, they are quick to say that, yes indeed, of course they're after capital growth. But a few more questions usually reveal that they never in fact considered the capital growth potential of the particular property that they acquired.

They 'knew' that property goes up in value, but didn't realise that that could mean anything from 20% per annum - to 2%: in other words, the difference between positive and *negative* growth in real terms (in excess of inflation). They based their choice of property not on capital growth potential but on all sorts of other factors: they liked the idea of rental income (perhaps guaranteed by the vendor), or tax deductions; they 'liked' the property; it was recommended by someone they trusted; it promised low maintenance costs; it looked like a 'bargain'; the finance offered to them on the property made it amazingly hassle-free.

None of these things make for capital growth. If you're looking to Wealth Build: look past them! **Focus on capital growth.** What is the property's history? What is its future?

Do you want to know what the single most important factor for capital growth is? *Land*. Land appreciates in value: buildings don't. However much you fall in love with a building, however low-maintenance it is, however much rent you can charge and however many deductions you can claim, the building will depreciate in value over time.

This is why so many investors get their fingers burnt with new units or townhouses. The land content of their investment may be only 10% of the purchase price, 90% of which is therefore a depreciating asset. This is the best-kept secret of the real estate industry - because what developer is going to tell you

> ## Do you want to know what the single most important factor for capital growth is? *Land*.

about it, when he can sell 20 units instead of a single house or duplex on the same block of land?

That's why you need to look behind the second veil: who are the people who are selling you the property - and what are they getting out of it?

The real estate industry itself ought to do some housekeeping, but it comes down to the old Latin principle *'caveat emptor'*: buyer beware! Ask yourself a few awkward questions about the competence and track record of anyone selling or recommending a property - and about their vested interests: what are they getting out of it?

You wouldn't believe, for example, how much heartache and loss of capital could be avoided by two simple questions.

- Ask the agent to disclose the commission and marketing fees that the vendor is paying. Commission used to be regulated, but is now open slather in most states. It's a useful reminder: however co-operative they appear, agents work for the vendor (and themselves) - *not* for you, the investing buyer. Their interests - and those of their clients - are served by securing the highest possible price for a property: yours, naturally, are not...

- Ask to see a copy of the bank's valuation of the property for security purposes. It is *not* always the same as the purchase price...

Sorry, but you cannot afford to be too trusting of the people you deal with. And that includes banks! Banks often lend on an investment property, knowing that the purchase price is way over their valuation of the property: they draw on your equity to make up the difference in the security - crippling your potential to build wealth. (Not that they disclose this to you! Some banks do have a policy to disclose their valuations, where there is a differential of more than 10%. This should be mandatory. It isn't. Some investors don't find out until a year or two later that they have an unexpected deficit in the calculation of their net worth.) I can assure you, banks would do things rather differently, if their right to recovery were limited to their valuation of the property!

Asking probing questions may be uncomfortable - but not nearly as uncomfortable as finding out that the equity you've built in your home over the past five to ten years has been wiped out because you didn't ask the questions...

> **Sorry, but you cannot afford to be too trusting of the people you deal with. And that includes banks!**

You need to listen carefully to the answers, too. Many of them may well come into the category of lies, damn' lies and statistics! For example, one of the tricks of the property trade is for marketers to justify sale prices and their claims of growth by quoting newspaper clippings and comparable investment sales. Companies have been selling units in Sydney for years, by claiming that there has been a 20-50% growth in the value of similar properties - based on what other investors had paid six, twelve or eighteen months before. But this is not a true reflection of the market. Investors aren't the true consumers of property - and what's to say that those previous investors weren't likewise talked into paying an over-inflated price?

Previous investment sales are often a barometer - not of local market conditions, but of the effectiveness of a slick sales operation. My own home ground, the Gold Coast, has probably got the 'best' operators in this style: they sell literally thousands of properties each year to would-be investors, at 10-30% over the market value, using comparable investment sales to justify their prices.

And this is another reason to steer clear of units for investment: 60-100% of all units built are sold to investors - not owner-occupiers. Which makes them a lousy barometer of market prices.

We'll discuss all these issues in detail, later in the book.

SO WHO AM I?

I'm asking you to look behind the veil of anyone who has an opinion about investment property. So, what are my qualifications?

Academically, none. But in 1985, when I was 22 years old, I started building a property portfolio that would have allowed me to retire very comfortably by the time I was 30. That in itself wouldn't make my advice better than the next guy's, but over the intervening period, I have bought myself literally thousands of properties, and now develop some three to five hundred residential properties per annum.

I have learned by experience how to create wealth - consistently - and how to use it sensibly. And I have successfully helped others to do the same.

In any case, I'm not trying to turn you into yet another 'expert' on property investment and management. I'd like to get you focused on capital growth, as a coach focuses a team on winning the game. I'd like to show you some of the pitfalls - so you don't have to fall foul of them the way I, and many others, did when we were starting out. And in the process, I may tell you a few things that don't usually get said in real estate circles...

Most importantly, I hope you'll realise that there are really *no* 'experts' when it comes to property investment. It's a bit like the weather: you can tell what it was like yesterday, and you might take an informed stab at forecasting what it'll be like tomorrow, based on current trends - but you know that conditions are changing from day to day and from place to place. The real 'expertise' is recognising that you're no expert - and staying on the ball.

Sceptics make the best Wealth Builders.

I don't expect you to take my word for anything. I'd like to give you the confidence to go out and ask questions, demand evidence, investigate further. You won't be able to eliminate all your doubts - or even all the risks: like any journey worth making, Wealth Building involves a few steps into unknown territory. But you can always test the ground. Sceptics make the best Wealth Builders.

SO THAT'S WHAT THIS BOOK IS ALL ABOUT

In Chapter 1, I start explaining in detail how you can build wealth. By the time you reach Chapter 11, you'll have absorbed a lot of information (although I hope it won't seem too much like hard work at the time). You may even have changed your thinking.

It's a real confidence booster to be able to see that happening. So please, take a minute to fill out the short quiz on page 23. You may already know some of the answers - but you may not. No worries, it's just like Wealth Building: you have to start somewhere! At the end of the book, you'll have the opportunity to do the quiz again. (And just like Wealth Building, you may be surprised how far you get!...)

Who is
John L Fitzgerald?

This is another 'Introduction' - this time to me, and how I learned about Wealth Building... The point is that I'm pretty much an average person: if anything, a bit below average academically, and a bit above average in sport. I recently bought a table tennis table ('flat packed for easy home assembly'). After half an hour wrestling with the instructions, I found a nearby 15 year old who put the whole thing together, as advertised, in about 3 minutes.

If I can build wealth, you can. Seriously. And if that's all you really need to know, feel free to skip the next few pages and go straight on to Part A!

I was born in Melbourne in 1963 and spent my first eight years in the middle-class suburb of Moorabbin. My father was a menswear retailer and went into business on his own at the age of 30. By the time he was 37 he had built up three menswear shops in Collingwood, Belgrave and Stawell. He was a devout Catholic from an Irish Catholic family: five children, all in Catholic schools. My mother ran the home full-time, having left a career as a ballroom dancing instructor to marry Dad.

The school holidays of September 1972 changed my life - all our lives - suddenly and forever. My oldest brother David (then aged 12) went, as we often did, to visit Uncle Morris's farm near Shepparton. We heard later that he and our cousin Peter were lighting a fire when David, who was practising his notorious balancing act on a log, lost his balance and fell into the fire. Uncle Morris got him to the hospital, where he was found to have third degree burns from knee to ankle, and given skin grafts. I remember visiting David at the Shepparton hospital, the slick lino floors and the cold concrete walls.

He was there for six weeks. And one Tuesday morning Dad drove out to visit him - and never returned. On his way home, the car had been sandwiched between two semi-trailers and driven off the road: he was killed instantly.

At nine years old, I sensed that there was a purpose behind those rollercoaster days: I believed that everything happens for a reason. That was the start of what I now see as a journey to discover my *own* purpose in the world - a journey which has since become linked to the creation and use of wealth. (If there's a 'bigger' purpose to your reading this book, I hope it will become clear as you read on...)

My mother had to take over the businesses, as well as run the family. She did a tremendous job, showing amazing business acumen for someone with no direct experience. To help her cope, we three boys were sent away to boarding school. I skipped Grade 6 in order to go to the same school as my brothers in 1974.

It was pretty clear from the first that I'd make my mark on the sports field, not in the classroom. I made the first 18 football team in Form 4 (Grade 10) despite being a year younger than my classmates, and I excelled in athletics and various other sports. All rather costly in terms of academic achievement... I left school in 1979, having just scraped enough of an aggregate to get my HSC. I was expected to go to university, or to repeat my HSC to improve my marks, but I had decided that the academic life wasn't for me. Boarding school makes you independent: I had hardly lived at home since I was 10 years old, and the sum total of my worldly possessions fitted into a locker 1.8 metres high by 40cm wide. It was time to 'get in amongst it' and see what life was all about.

A friend and I had planned to hitchhike to Queensland (I wasn't old enough to have a car, being not quite 17).

In January 1980, the friend pulled out - and I packed a knapsack and headed off alone for the Gold Coast.

The Gold Coast was in the midst of a property boom, and I immediately knew I wanted to be a part of it. I applied for several real estate positions as a salesman and eventually, through contacts, got a start with Bert Cockerel, who had an office in Surfers Paradise. To call Bert a 'Jack of all trades' would be an understatement. I remember going round to visit a motel he owned on the highway in Surfers, called the Golden Sun Motel - which is now the site of a 30-storey highrise tower called Zenith. He also owned the picture theatre at Palm Beach - and was an avid fisherman, who used to do the fishing report on the local radio station! A great guy.

> **The Gold Coast was in the midst of a property boom, and I immediately knew I wanted to be a part of it.**

I went round to see him about signing my application for a licence as a real estate salesman. I had to disclose to him that I wasn't yet 17, but Bert wasn't phased by technicalities - and neither, it seemed, was whoever rubber stamped the application forms: despite being up-front about my date of birth, I was duly and officially licenced for real estate sales. (Does that make me the youngest ever...? Perhaps it's better not to ask.)

Less than a year after I joined Bert, I was introduced to George Margolis, who had built a fortune in real estate during the 1960s - and lost it in the crash of 1974-75. Now, he was re-emerging from bankruptcy, and he had a good plan: with his knowledge and contacts, and my energy, we would make a tremendous partnership. So at 17 and 9 months,

I became an associate partner of Cousins Real Estate. I still didn't know anything about real estate. Fortunately, I was a fast learner.

These were the heady days of the early '80s: looking back, 'incredible' is the word that comes to mind. At my age and with my experience (neither one particularly impressive), I could advertise for people willing to invest in a private property trust to develop units - and secure literally dozens of investors who were prepared to punt $50,000 or $100,000 on my ability to acquire a site, build a building and make a profit. Like I say: 'incredible'.

> # Fortunately, I was a fast learner.

Of course, it wasn't just 'my ability': I had the building advice of a structural engineer who was part of the management team - and, of course, George Margolis.

BOOMS AND BUSTS - AND BAD DECISIONS

I remember all too well the highrise buildings going up along Old Burleigh Road and the Surfers Paradise strip, where units would be settling in a building such as Aquarius. The developer would attend settlement, only to see the property transferred two or three times - on the spot!

Greed, as ever, was the underlying factor: real estate agents were promising that if speculators bought, they could on-sell the unit immediately, because of the sky-high demand. It was not uncommon to see units, sold off the plan by the developer for $150,000 - $180,000, re-sell for $250,000, then $400,000, then $500,000 at settlement! (I call this the Bigger

Fool Theory: if you invest in real estate on this basis, you have to be sure there's a bigger fool than you coming along behind, to give you a back door...)

> I call this the Bigger Fool Theory: if you invest in real estate on this basis, you have to be sure there's a bigger fool than you coming along behind...

On the heels of greed, as ever, came the crash. In 1982, you couldn't *give* highrise units away for love or money! Literally tens of millions of dollars were wiped off the (over-inflated) prices paid by investors at the height of the feeding frenzy.

Developers also had their problems, notably Dainford Ltd, which had built most of the highrise on the Gold Coast and had just completed the Peninsula building, the tallest and one of the best located buildings in Surfers Paradise. A record number of people had acquired the units on the basis that they could sell them on, found they couldn't - and defaulted at settlement.

The ups and downs of the early 1980s taught me a lesson very quickly: real estate is an ever-changing market - and while buildings are its prime 'product', it's the *land* that is the true, limited commodity. People repeatedly made the mistake of paying a premium above already over-inflated prices for a *building* - which in itself was commonplace and easily replaceable.

Things haven't changed much: speculators are still madly snapping up inner-city units in Melbourne and Sydney, despite one in five currently having to take a *loss* on re-sale! (What percentage of Australians do you think buy units to live in, as owner-occupiers? Take a guess.)*

Just 6%!

BECOMING A WEALTH BUILDER

I acquired my first house and land package in Shailer Park, Brisbane, in 1985 for the tidy sum of $49,000. I borrowed approximately $47,000 on it - which sounded like a lot of money in those days. But that meant I could start out with just $2,000 of my own money - and today that property is worth $140,000. That's where I started.

I had cottoned on to the fact that it was land that appreciated in value, not buildings, and that this created some rather encouraging mathematical effects: namely, if the house goes up by 10%, the land will go up by 20%. Armed with this information, and with a couple of houses under my belt, in 1987 I approached one of Australia's largest developers, Dainford Limited, and asked them to finance me into land estates. Dainford generally took 'long positions' in the market (that is, committed to projects which wouldn't provide income for 3-5 years), so my formula for acquiring land and immediately turning it into income was pretty attractive.

Our first project together was a 1,200 lot estate at Loganholme, south of Brisbane, which we acquired as an *englobo* parcel (before subdivision and infrastructure development) for approximately $2,500 per lot. Lots in that area at that stage were selling for around $25,000, and houses for around $60,000. As house values crept up to over $140,000, the raw land value rocketed to $90,000, forcing the *englobo* land up to approximately $40,000 - $50,000.

This sounds like a complete sweetheart deal, but for Wealth Building purposes, I wouldn't recommend it: land on its own generates no regular income (unlike a rentable property) and despite the potential for super profits, roughly 9 out of 10 land developers go broke in any 10 year period. I was one of the lucky ones.

In four years, Dainford and I developed and sold over 1,000 properties together. Yet, for all that activity, I realised I would have been a lot wealthier a lot sooner if I had constructed *homes* on 10% of the allotments that I developed and sold, and kept them as rental properties...

Over ten years of buying and managing and selling investment properties, I probably made most of the mistakes that can be made - although I like to think I avoided a *few*, through seeing them coming. I gathered a pretty good idea of what makes a good investment, and how to make a good investment work better. I realised that you don't have to be a property developer to build wealth in property. (In fact, rather the reverse: most of them go broke at one time or another, pushing for bigger and bigger projects.)

Since 1994, my company, the JLF Corporation, has worked on a system - based on the structure outlined in this book - to facilitate Wealth Building Programmes for 'ordinary' Australians. (None of them ever turns out to be 'ordinary'...) More recently, this work has been backed up by public seminars on Wealth Building for anyone who is curious about the concept.

From the start, we set out to do things a little differently to other developers and marketing operations we knew. We chose to build a relationship with our clients, beginning with their first property purchase. We've worked with those clients over the years, monitoring their capital growth and guiding them step by step to establishing a property portfolio. (Unfortunately, such a relationship is not possible with some organisations - not for their lack of willingness, but for their clients' lack of sufficient equity growth to make the second property purchase...)

It's been fascinating for me to see people come fresh to the idea of Wealth Building, and to see where they get to. Some of the people we work with are top sports people, who need to reduce their tax liabilities and shift their thinking from 'income' to 'wealth' for a future beyond sport. Others are those 'ordinary' Australians, who might never have thought beyond paying off their own home and earning a decent salary until they retire - but for whom the words 'financial freedom' (or is it 'millionaire'?) conjure up a whole new world.

BECOMING A CUSTODIAN

And there's another dimension to it, for me. Whatever our clients' initial motivation to build wealth - and I guess we all start out 'self-centred' about this to some extent - I've watched person after person achieve more than wealth through the journey. Many have also found perspective and purpose: definitely, more-than-financial rewards.

I had my own major shift in thinking along the way. As you may have gathered, I knew from a pretty early age that I wanted to be wealthy: I set some ambitious goals for myself, and went after them aggressively. I got there - and then found that my perspective had changed.

There are very few wealthy people in the world. *Very* few. And I believe that it's pretty much up to those who control and enjoy the world's wealth to help those who don't! Once I had pulled myself into the former category, I felt the weight of that responsibility. I say 'weight', but I've actually found that the opportunity to use my wealth responsibly - to make a contribution to society - is one of the most joyful and enriching experiences of my life.

In 1990, I met a husband and wife psychologist team - Ron and Suwanti Farmer - and together we established the Toogoolawa Children's Home. Some of the wealth I have created now funds full-time residential care for homeless and troubled youth, an extraordinary school, and outreach programs in the Brisbane area. I love the fact that my contribution can be the small difference that makes a big difference in these kids' lives - and so, I believe, in the future of Australia.

That's an important part of my story. I think it's an important part of Wealth Building, too, and when we help people to build wealth, we are not shy of urging them to think of themselves as *custodians* - as well as creators - of wealth that can make a difference in the world.

That's why, in 1998, we changed the name of our business, and now call ourselves - as we see ourselves - the Custodian Wealth Builders Group.

We express our corporate mission and philosophy quite simply. And we encourage each Wealth Builder who joins us to become a fellow Custodian.

Purpose:	To create wealth
	To serve humanity
Integrity:	To accept responsibility
Truth:	To keep questioning

Of course, none of this may be important to you right now. Feel free to put it all aside, just in a corner of your mind somewhere. Start building wealth for yourself and your family, to meet your future needs - or to set yourself a challenge. And as you build your wealth, and meet your goals, perhaps you'll remember this seed that I've sown. Perhaps you too will find something more.

On that note, let's move on to the business of building wealth!

PART A
Starting points

Start-up Quiz

The following are just a few questions to help us focus on Wealth Building, and to remind us where we are starting from. Don't worry if you don't know the answers yet: you will, by the time you attempt this as a Round-up Quiz at the end of the book!

1. In making a Wealth Building investment decision, what would be more important?

   ☐ How you felt about it

   ☐ How it stacked up logically

2. What has shown the higher investment return over the last 10 years?

   ☐ Shares

   ☐ Residential property

3. In buying a residential investment property for Wealth Building, what would be more important?

   ☐ Rental returns

   ☐ Taxation benefits

   ☐ Capital growth

4. If you invested in residential property, would you use the same criteria and decision-making process that you used to acquire your own home?

   ☐ Yes   ☐ No

5. Is it prudent for me to acquire property close to where I live?

☐ Yes   ☐ No

6. What would be more important in acquiring an investment property for *Wealth Building?*

☐ Managing your cash flow

☐ Buying the right property

7. What type of property would show the highest capital growth?

☐ Unit/townhouse

☐ House

☐ Land

8. If you had $50,000 deposit to invest in property, would you be better off buying:

☐ One property for $100,000?

☐ One property for $300,000?

☐ Two properties for $150,000 each?

9. Have a guess at the average house price in your capital city in the following years.

1999 $ _____

1989 $ _____

1979 $ _____

10. Which institution(s) effectively control the affordability of housing in Australia?

☐ Real Estate Institute ☐ Banks

☐ Property Developers ☐ Valuers

11. Is the number of renters of property in Australia:

☐ Increasing? ☐ Decreasing?

12. Approximately what is the PAYE Income Tax on a salary of $45,000? $ _____

13. Can I use my PAYE tax to build wealth?

☐ Yes ☐ No

14. What is the maximum percentage you can borrow from a bank (a) on an investment property? and (b) on shares (without a margin call)?

(a) _____ % (b) _____ %

15. Which would be the better of these two properties to purchase for wealth building?

(a)   A 'period' home close to the city with 70% land content for $200,000; or

(b)   A brand new home 15kms from the city with 50% land content?

Sorry, but I'm not going to give you the answers at this point! That's what the book is for. Forget about this Quiz altogether, for the time being.

At the end of the book, you'll get to tackle the same questions again. With answers provided - if, by that time, you need them...

Chapter 1:
Why Build
Wealth?

DO YOU WANT TO BE WEALTHY?

Silly question, right? *Everybody* wants to be wealthy. Imagine the security and the freedom. Imagine retiring with enough money to do all the things you've wanted to do, for as many years as you've got - and not having to rely on the government for a cent!

It seems extraordinary, but when we surveyed 2,200 people in the south-west Brisbane area, 78% of them said they 'never thought about building wealth'.

Let's look at it another way.

How much do you reckon you'd need - per year - to live comfortably in retirement? I'm not asking you to do budgets and calculations and adjustments for inflation (although at some stage, if you're talking to an investment advisor, it would be a good idea). I'm just talking ball-park figures: what kind of a sum per year would you want to retire on, in today's dollars?

> **Nearly all of us want to be wealthy - and nearly all of us retire below the poverty line! What's going on?**

Most of the people I talk to would say $30,000 - $40,000 per annum.

Your own estimate: $_____.

That estimate may be perfectly realistic for your own financial circumstances: you'd have to do a few calculations to find out. But the following chart shows what Australians actually *do* retire on.

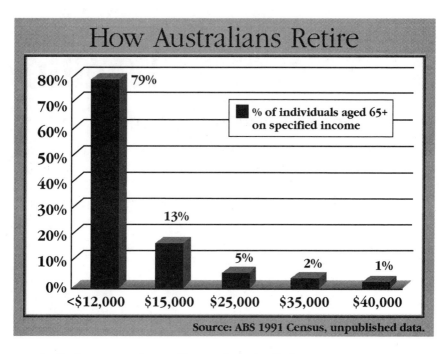

How Australians Retire

% of individuals aged 65+ on specified income

	<$12,000	$15,000	$25,000	$35,000	$40,000
%	79%	13%	5%	2%	1%

Source: ABS 1991 Census, unpublished data.

Nearly all of us want to be wealthy - and nearly all of us retire below the poverty line! What's going on?

To retire on $38,000 per annum, you actually need around $800,000 in assets, *and* to own your own home.

And that's in today's dollars. In 20 years' time, with inflation at 4%, the equivalent sum would be $80,000 per year, requiring $1.6 million in assets.

How many of us have a plan in place to build up those kinds of assets by the time we retire? Apparently, only 1 in 100 of us! If you are one of those, please accept my congratulations and best wishes, and feel free to stop reading (although there may be a few things in this book that will surprise even you...). If you are *not* one of those, it's *your* responsibility to change this for yourself! (Think about it. On whom would you want to be financially dependent when you retire? The government? Your kids? Read on...)

WHY AREN'T MORE AUSTRALIANS WEALTHY?

There are a number of answers to this question. (I haven't included 'waiting to win the Lottery' - although, with $75 billion 'invested' in gambling in Australia each year, you'd think we were pretty serious about this as a retirement plan!)

We don't have enough money to build wealth

Wrong. The structure I'll show you in this book allows you - even encourages you - to start small. You only need a combined annual gross income of $35,000, and a small amount of cash or equity in your own home or other property, to get started. Wealth is accessible to most Australians. Mostly, it's about using the resources you have, and restructuring your cash flow. And all that takes is (a) knowing how and (b) choosing to give it a go.

Our parents never taught us to build wealth

Most people my age were taught that we would grow up, get a trade or a university degree and then a job: we'd save up enough money for a deposit on a house, and we'd use our work income to pay off the loan on that house over 25 years - and *then* maybe we could consider another investment. Sound familiar? Well, that's exactly what most Australians do.

I call this 'income thinking'. We need to replace it with 'capital thinking', as we'll see below.

There's always a safety net

I think this is part of the same thing. Our grandparents seemed to live fairly happily on the pension in the post-war years, and in the '50s and '60s Australia enjoyed a relatively high standard of living compared to other nations. Of course, that was when there were about 18 taxpayers for every pensioner. Today, there are less than 6 taxpayers per pensioner, and if demographic trends continue, within 20 years there will be less than one taxpayer per pensioner. Meanwhile, because we're living longer, the average Australian will have to fund at least 20 years of retirement.

It won't be long before the government simply won't be able to afford the age pension - even at its current meager levels. So we might like to think about making our own arrangements...

We don't like debt

This is something else our parents taught us. There are some sound values behind it - self-reliance, pay your own way - and it's true that escalating debt is a concern. But we need to distinguish between debt on consumer items that depreciate in value (like a car, a dining suite,

Today there are less than six taxpayers per pensioner. In 20 years...

or a stereo system) and borrowing on an asset that *appreciates in value* and *generates income* (like property). The latter kind of debt (a) supports the borrower's ability to make the necessary repayments, and (b) offers a profit on sale of the asset.

On the other hand, you could buy a new BMW cabriolet (say) for $100,000, and by the time you drive it out of the showroom, it's only worth $85,000: if you borrowed $100,000 on it, you're already facing a deficit of $15,000, which you have to pay off. Each year, more of the same: you could end up making payments of $12,000 for four years - and still face a balloon payment of about $70,000 (which may, or may not, equal the capital value of the car by that time). Now, *that's* debt...

Ironically, people routinely run up thousands of dollars in 'small' debts on consumer items - but baulk at taking on a mortgage.

Let's get debt into perspective. You can't build wealth without acquiring substantial assets for capital growth - and you can't, realistically, do that without borrowing the money to invest: that is,'*gearing*'.

It's an income world

What does 'being wealthy' mean to you? Some people might say: a big salary, with a lifestyle to match. But that's not how wealth works. Income doesn't by itself make you wealthy. You spend some. You save some (maybe), and inflation gradually wears its value away. Capital, on the other hand, is material wealth which can be used to produce more wealth, by investment. Capital grows, income flows (mostly, through your fingers...)

Unfortunately, most people don't get past income: they don't get their money growing and working for them. The system is there - but only capital-focused people use it to build wealth.

You can't *save* your way to wealth.

Wealth Building is strictly for whizz-kids

Some investment advisors would like you to think so. But the good news is that property investment need not be the sole preserve of financial experts. By the end of this book, you'll know enough about 'leverage' and 'negative gearing' to get by. You'll have a simple investment structure and clear principles to work with. And if the whole business seems like too much of a hassle - remember, you don't have to do it all yourself! You can get advice and help with everything from working out an initial budget to managing a whole portfolio of investment properties.

Custodian Wealth Builders are just one example of an organisation that offers a whole range of services in the property investment field, or you could get advice from other sources. Look behind the veil. Try and find someone who has actually done what they are advising you to do! This goes for accountants, financial advisers and real estate agents: there are some good ones who have built wealth - and that's the first credential I'd look for.

Wealth Building is strictly for sharks

It's easy to get that impression - and not everybody relates to the idea that 'Greed is Good' the way we seemed to when Michael Douglas said it in the movie *Wall Street* in the early '80s.

I think we need to challenge the way we think about what wealth is for. Sure, it's about quality lifestyle, providing for family, a financially secure retirement, control over your future and all that good stuff. But it is also about *responsibility*.

As I outlined in my personal story, the 'custodian' philosophy

> ## Sharing in the custodianship of our society's future is one way of being all you can be

is that those few of us who are fortunate and informed enough to build wealth can - and must - choose to use it responsibly. Wealth puts us in a position to help those in trouble and need - and to shape the kind of fair and hopeful society we would want our children to inherit. It's also our responsibility to educate the next generation to manage and preserve capital, for our nation's financial and social well-being. Custodian Wealth Builders believe that this is what true investment in the future means - and we find that it yields the most valuable and satisfying returns.

We encourage all fellow Wealth Builders to adopt this philosophy. This book is about what's possible - in all sorts of ways. Sharing in the custodianship of our society's future is one way of being all you can be.

WHAT'S THE SOLUTION?

At the risk of sounding like a sportswear advertisement, it's quite simple.

Just think differently!

JUST THINK DIFFERENTLY:
CAPITAL, NOT INCOME.

When we talk about 'Wealth Building', we are talking about:

- establishing a *structure,* or system, to manage your cash flow

- to acquire *assets* (in this case, residential real estate)

- for *capital growth:* that is, to increase the value of your investment over time.

Your investment may, of course, also offer you income and tax advantages. But it's the capital growth that counts. It's the capital growth that makes millionaires.

And as it happens, most millionaires achieve capital growth by investing in real estate.

This book will take you step by step through how it all works, and what you have to do.

Chapter 2:
Why residential real estate?

If you just look at results, you'd have to say that property seems to make good investment sense.

For example, it is, consistently, a major source of wealth for the wealthiest Australians. (And 90% of millionaires worldwide.)

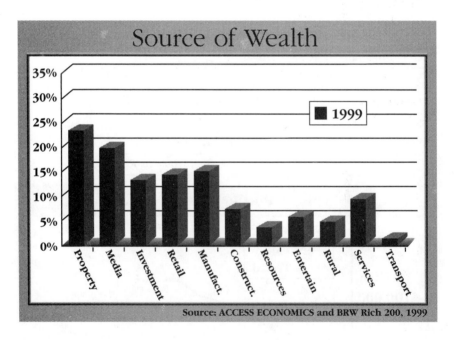

Source: ACCESS ECONOMICS and BRW Rich 200, 1999

Residential real estate, in particular, scores pretty high on just about any quality you'd look for in an investment - remembering that your purpose is capital growth.

☑ SECURITY

Residential real estate offers the security of 'bricks and mortar' compared to the fluctuating values of shares and commodities - and even compared to the manageability of commercial and industrial properties, over the medium to long term. Even allowing for the ups and downs in real estate values that we all hear about, the underlying trend shows remarkably steady growth.

You can see this trend quite clearly in the following table and graph showing house prices over the last 30-40 years.

House prices 1978 - 1998					
	Melbourne	Sydney	Brisbane	Adelaide	Perth
	$	$	$	$	$
1978	40,200	46,000	30,500	32,800	35,200
1988	113,000	178,300	74,900	80,800	78,000
1998	195,000	258,100	140,000	120,300	142,900
					Source: REIA.

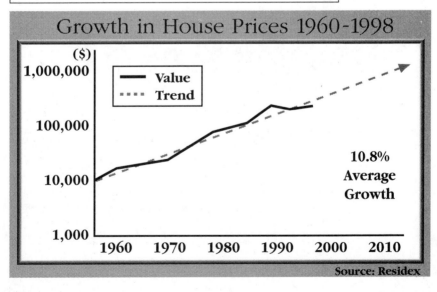

In fact, the growth pattern has stayed pretty constant throughout the century.

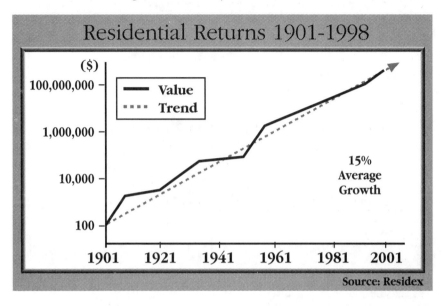

Residential Returns 1901-1998

15% Average Growth

Source: Residex

Roughly speaking, this means that residential property has historically *doubled in value every 8 - 10 years*. And don't forget that as the population continues to grow, the demand for housing must continue to increase.

☑ PERFORMANCE

Residential real estate offers significant return on your investment. A report by ANZ Managed Funds showed that, over a 10 year period (measured from 1989 - 1999), the median house price kept up with other returns.

And these are just averages. The better your real estate investment strategy is - where you buy, what you buy, how much land content and how you finance — the better the returns can be. Remember median house price doesn't take into account shrinking lot size over the last 10-20 years (*see Foreword viii*).

10 Year Investment Returns as at 31st March 1999

	% Returns
Superannuation Funds	10.9%
Gold Bullion	-0.6%
Cash	8.1%
Residential Property	9.1%
Fixed Interest	12.5%
International Shares	14.3%
Australian Shares	12.1%

Source: ANZ Bank

☑ LEVERAGE

Because of its security and performance, residential real estate also represents 'security' (in the legal/financial sense) or collateral for loans. Most banks regard residential real estate as prime security, against which some will lend up to 90-95% of the property's value.

Definition
Gearing is borrowing money for investment.

'Leverage' in mechanics is a way of turning a small amount of force, at a strategic point, into a much greater force. (Think of a car jack.) Financial leverage works the same way: you can use a small amount of money to acquire an asset of much higher value, on which you reap larger returns and growth. (This is a key factor in the performance of property, as compared to shares, as a long term investment. We'll look at this in more detail, below.)

Definition

Leverage is gearing your investment so that the proportion of capital you invest is low in relation to borrowings: say, 20% : 80%, or 10% : 90%.

Equity is your 'net worth': the value of assets that is actually yours, or accessible to you: in other words, the value of your assets *minus* the debt you owe on them.

If the value of an investment property goes up, and the mortgage on it stays constant, your equity - or 'net worth' - increases.

Basically, the high degree of leverage on residential property allows you to build wealth by using just a little of your own money - and quite a lot of other people's!

You don't have to be wealthy to build wealth!

This is great news, because it means you don't have to be wealthy to build wealth! Residential real estate is actually one of the most *affordable* investments around.

The banks' confidence in residential property allows you to use your increased equity as security in a fairly liberal way, to piggy-back one purchase on another and build up a portfolio of properties - as we'll show you in Chapter 3.

WHAT ABOUT SHARES?

A lot of people will try to tell you that shares are a better investment than property. It's true that some shares show a higher income return. They are easily tradeable, and shares in the major companies have the advantage of high liquidity: they're practically cash. Shares have shown good capital growth, too, especially over the last ten to fifteen years - although both camps seem to be able to produce convincing historical information showing capital growth of 7% - 15% per annum. (In fact, the Australian All Ordinaries share index *averaged* just under 9% over the last 30 years.)

The difference is the *leverage*. You can buy property on a 10% deposit, because it represents a bankable security. When it comes to shares, however, most banks will only lend 50-60% of the purchase value.

Here's an example. Bill and Ted both have $20,000 in cash. Bill puts his down as a deposit on a property, while Ted uses his to buy shares.

Let's use the ANZ figures and assume that in the first year, the value of Bill's property increases by 9.1% - and Ted's shares go up by 12.1% Which was the better investment?

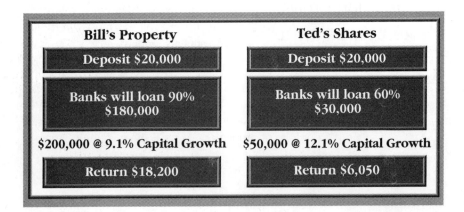

Bill's Property	Ted's Shares
Deposit $20,000	Deposit $20,000
Banks will loan 90% $180,000	Banks will loan 60% $30,000
$200,000 @ 9.1% Capital Growth	$50,000 @ 12.1% Capital Growth
Return $18,200	Return $6,050

Bill gets 3 times a better return in property.

Bill's *equity* has gone up from $20,000 to $38,200 ($218,200 - $180,000). That's a return of just under 100%.

Ted's equity has gone up from $20,000 to $26,050 ($56,050 - $30,000): a 30% return.

So even if the shares have twice the 'growth' factor, the property offers more than twice the growth in true capital worth (equity) - simply because of its leveraging ability.

> **Even if the shares have twice the 'growth' factor, the property offers more than twice the growth in true capital worth (equity) - simply because of its leveraging ability.**

Property's reliability makes a difference, too. When banks lend on shares, they usually reserve the right to a *margin call* should the shares drop in value. (A margin call is where you are required to provide a cash top-up to maintain the agreed loan-to-security-value ratio. So if you borrowed 50% of the value of shares, and their price dropped, you would have to pay off part of the loan so that the outstanding amount still represented only 50% of the value of the shares.) This can be scary, because some banks can give you just two or three days to rectify: if you have a falling share price, you could be topping up on a daily basis!

Banks *don't,* however, require a margin call on 3-5 year loans on property - so there's no risk of them selling you up because of a temporary hiccup or glitch in the market!

WHAT ABOUT COMMERCIAL PROPERTY?

'Commercial' property includes land and premises used for retail, offices, industry, entertainment and hospitality: anything from the corner store to the Westfield Centre. While residential property values are expected to maintain their rising trend, the future for commercial and industrial property is much less certain - and that's generally reflected in the amount banks are willing to lend. Morever, while the growing demand for rental property allows you to be a relatively passive investor in residential housing, you can't take the same kind of back seat with commercial property.

When you buy a commercial property, you're buying land plus buildings plus *goodwill*. If the property is tenanted, its purchase price will generally be based on the rate of capital return it offers - which may be a far cry from the building's replacement value. Let me give you an example. A friend of mine used to develop Big Rooster (now Red Rooster) outlets. He purchased the land for around $80,000 and built the premises for around $100,000, with car parking and landscaping and so on. He then leased it to Big Rooster for a whopping $40-45,000 per annum, and sold on - showing a 10% return. This is good development business.

The point is that an investor buying a Big Rooster outlet is paying a premium of $200,000 for goodwill - in effect, for Big Rooster's continued success. But if Big Rooster left those premises at the end of the lease, you would be left with an empty shell, with a replacement value half of what you paid for it, and limited ability to attract new tenants, since it was purpose-built for a particular fast food chain...

Businesses come and go - and not just geographically. You only have to think about the retail areas around you. The last 10 - 15 years have seen a mushrooming of regional shopping centres, which have all but squeezed out the strip shops and neighbourhood shopping centres. They come complete with entertainment and refreshment facilities, so you can stay all day - and pick up a few more impulse buys. With the advent of 24-hour shopping, it seems only a matter of time before the regional centres and the petrol station 'convenience stores' take over completely.

Businesses come and go - and not just geographically.

Then there's the Internet. How might it affect our day-to-day shopping and communication patterns? It is certainly conceivable that in 10 - 15 years' time, we could be doing all of our grocery shopping from home, and paying by credit card. We've already got the less high-tech version of the same phenomenon: department stores and speciality shops sell billions of dollars of goods around the world via TV advertising and home catalogues, eliminating the need for stock-holding and retail outlets.

What this adds up to is the disappearance of small retail businesses, or their inability to pay commercial rents - and therefore vacant commercial properties. You see them everywhere. And vacancy is particularly bad news for commercial property, because loss of income also means loss of value.

At the time of writing, the big regional shopping centres are planning to float off parts or all of their real estate portfolio, but this could be an equally dangerous investment over the next 10-15 years. Inflation is low and shop-keepers are struggling to pay even today's rents. Quite bluntly, shopping centres are sold on their potential for rental return - so if the rents aren't going up, neither is the value of the property. Add to that the rapidly-approaching saturation point of areas such as the Gold Coast (which already has twice as much retail space *per capita* as any other location in Australia) and you might say there was a serious problem looming.

It's pretty much the same with industrial investments, given the decline in heavy manufacturing, and the increasing use of technology. Office premises are also shrinking, as the traditional functions of the office are revolutionised. Typing pools have been all but replaced by scanners and voice-activated wordprocessors, and mail rooms by touch-of-a-button world-wide e-mail. Nearly everything can be done from home, with computer and telecommunications link-ups: 'telecommuting' is already a reality in many businesses, small and large. (It amazes me to think that back in 1984, I hardly knew what a mobile phone was...)

> ## At least you *know* you know how to choose and buy a home...

THE FUTURE FOR HOUSING, HOWEVER...

Fortunately, we all have to live somewhere. And the wonders of modern technology still haven't provided any alternative to living in some form of 'housing'. (Indeed 'houses' are still the norm, outside medium- to high-density urban areas.)

AREN'T WE ALREADY INVESTING IN RESIDENTIAL REAL ESTATE?

One of the things I like about residential real estate is that it is a known quantity for a lot of people. They may not be entirely comfortable with the language of finance and banking, leverage and gearing, but they have *some* experience of the sector, especially if they own their own home. This can be pretty reassuring, if you're sticking your toe in the shark-infested waters of investment for the first time: at least you *know* you know how to choose and buy a home...

Sorry, but actually this makes for rotten investment decisions!

It's a bit like taking up snow skiing.

If you haven't snow skiied, it's a great sport - and if it's accessible to you, I recommend that you give it a try. I learned some of the basic principles when I was a kid, but only took it up again about five years ago, having water-skiied for many years. And now, on my annual visit to the snowfields in Victoria or New South Wales, I'm constantly reminded of two things.

1. Snow skiing and water skiing may look vaguely similar, but if you try to snow ski the same way you water ski - you end up on your face (or worse). The apparent familiarity makes you feel pleasantly confident, but it can also blind you to the fact that the principles and techniques involved are quite different.

2. Logic and emotion can give you two conflicting messages - and if you're doing something that 'feels' risky, it's the feelings that shout loudest! When you're on top of a mountain, thinking about heading down, logic and science and the ski instructor and all those good things are

telling you that to stay in complete control, you need to lean down the mountain, with all your weight on your downhill leg. Meanwhile, your emotions are telling you to keep your bum as close to the snow as humanly possible! It's easy to say 'go with the logic', and I'm the first to admit that, for a novice, hurtling down a mountain at 30-40 kph doesn't feel 'in control' at all: and, yes, the temptation to lean cautiously back into the slope is fairly powerful. But that's the reason you see me, and a fair few others, losing control on the slopes and ending up with our bums *on* the snow. We let emotion, not logic or science, make our decisions for us.

Logic and emotion can give you two conflicting messages

And that's exactly how too many people invest in real estate. They take the (largely emotional) experience they have in choosing their home, and try to apply it to choosing an investment property. Logic and science go out the window - and so does capital growth.

So what *are* the right criteria to use?

CHOOSING A HOME

When we choose somewhere to live, we naturally go with our emotions, gut instincts and lifestyle choices, and quite rightly: this is going to be our home. We walk into a place with our partner, having looked at several properties - perhaps not even knowing what exactly we're looking for - and suddenly we're in love. It's the place of our dreams (or looks like it could be, with a little work).

I had exactly the same experience buying the property where I currently live. My fiancée and I had been looking for months, and because of our lifestyle we particularly wanted acreage land near water. On a rainy Saturday afternoon, I drove up the driveway of perhaps the twentieth property I'd looked at. I got out of the car and knew instantly: this was the one. I made an offer on the place before I was halfway through the front door - and without even consulting my fiancée. (Talk about risky decision-making...) Fortunately, she had exactly the same response to the place when we went back together the next morning - and of course, we did eventually get around to going through cupboards, flicking switches and checking carpets.

I've since pulled down that house and built another one, and I'm the first to admit that I completely overcapitalised on the place as an investment. Even so, it was a great way to buy and make a home! If you're happy in your own place - be happy. You need to 'feel at home' where you live: it makes a huge difference to your work and other areas of your life.

But it's not the way to invest in residential real estate for capital growth.

CHOOSING AN INVESTMENT PROPERTY... NOT!

I always seem to get people coming up to me, bragging that they've started 'Wealth Building', and all excited because they've just purchased an investment property to take advantage of negative gearing, et cetera, et cetera. They sound like they've won lotto - and they want to tell me all about it.

They spoke to their accountant and bank manager, got the tick, and went off in search of a property. Their first port of call was the local real estate agent, because after all, they'd purchased their home through him, and they'd got chummy over the years. And would you *believe* it? The Perfect Property had just come on the market - Just Around the Corner from their home! Old Mrs Reid's house was for sale: she was moving into a retirement village - signed a contract to purchase a unit. It was such a big house, and she couldn't look after it any more. And what a *bargain!* ('She's asking $300,000, but I'm sure if you made a cash offer you could get it for $285,000...')

> **Does that sound like a dumb reason? It does, if your purpose is to build wealth.**

Our couple can't believe their luck. They've driven past Old Mrs Reid's house a thousand times, always admired it, and now they not only get the chance to buy it - they can get it for a full $15,000 discount on asking price! Within 30 days, they've got themselves an investment property...

Why did they choose this particular property? "It's ideal: *we can drive by it every day on our way home from work!*"

Does that sound like a dumb reason? It does, if your purpose is to build wealth. (In fact, our couple has broken just about every rule in this book...)

And do people really *do* that? It sure looks like it. Of the Australians who own residential investment properties:

*** 26% INVEST WITHIN THEIR OWN POSTCODE!**

CHOOSING A PROPERTY FOR CAPITAL GROWTH

Here's where the logic and science come in. There are three questions we need to ask ourselves, if we want to invest in residential real estate for capital growth.

1. *What **structure** will best utilise my cash resources to allow me to build up a property portfolio in the shortest period of time?*

2. *What **sort of property** will give me the highest capital growth?*

3. *What **location** will give me the highest capital growth?*

Unfortunately, most Australians who invest in property don't ask themselves even *one* of those questions - let alone all three - which is why 97% of them don't maximise their capital growth or their tax benefits. And why only 1% of them build enough wealth to retire on an income (in today's terms) of more than $40,000 per annum...

Just one more statistic: less than 13% of all property investors buy more than one property. But *one* property won't make you wealthy. You need to focus on building a *portfolio* of five or six properties over 10 years. The good news is, this catapults you to the very top - that magic 1% - of successful investors in financial security and freedom.

So it's time to ask - and answer - the three big questions. We'll start with structure, in Chapter 3.

Chapter 3:
A structure
for growth

In order to build wealth, you need to:

- establish a structure
- to acquire assets
- for capital growth.

Why do you need a 'structure'? You need a structure because there are a number of elements involved in making your investment work. You've got land and buildings, equity and loans, tax and tax benefits, rental income and outlays, time. The mix and balance of all these elements needs to be just right in order to *accelerate portfolio development* and *maximise capital growth* - and it needs to be do-able time and time again. If you can work out what the 'best fit' is, and set it out as a simple formula, you can achieve predictable results - without having to juggle all the balls in the air all the time!

Building wealth using property is a bit like building muscle using weights.

There are a number of elements to building muscle.

The weights are only the *'vehicle'* you use to build the muscle. (Some people seem to think just owning weights is good for you - but it's using them, and how you use them, that counts.)

Technique is important. You need to use a weight that is within your capacity, and to lift it correctly, in order to stretch a specific muscle. Then you can gradually build up to heavier weights. Gyms are full of aspiring body-builders lifting weights that are far too big for them, so they have to use their back or some other part of their body to assist the lift: they are not effectively working the muscle they are trying to build, and they risk injury and unproductive down time.

Diet is all-important to 'fuel' the exercise. You need the basic energy of carbohydrates, a reduced fat intake, and an increased intake of protein, for specific muscle growth.

Finally, *rest* is essential. The muscle actually only grows when resting after being stretched. As the sport has grown more scientific in recent years, body builders who might have worked on a daily or 48-hour basis are now being taught to work each muscle group just one to three times a fortnight, for maximum growth.

A weekly or fortnightly exercise routine incorporating all these factors would provide an efficient, effective structure to follow.

Start small, think big!

OK, SO BACK TO WEALTH BUILDING!

An effective structure for Wealth Building will incorporate the same kind of elements.

- A 'vehicle' for building wealth: in this case, residential real estate. The land is the vehicle for capital growth, and the building, for generating rental income.
- A 'technique' which will maximise the effectiveness of the vehicle for your purpose of capital growth. You need to select a suitable vehicle: the right property, in the right location. And you need to start - and stay - within your financial capacity: at the bottom end of general affordability, where most people can afford a first property. As you see growth, you can begin to build up a portfolio: more properties, not more expensive ones.
- 'Fuel' for your investment. With a basic level of available equity and income, you can secure *finance*. With the right property and the right lender, you can borrow 90% of the purchase price. You put in just 10% of the capital - and access 100% of the capital growth. That's the beauty of leverage.

> ## You're setting things up so that there's a lot to gain - and not a lot to lose.

In order to make this work, without draining your personal resources, you need *income* from the property, to service the debt. If you optimise the rental income and maximise the tax benefits available, you can effectively offset *all* your outlays: not just the loan interest, but also maintenance, rates, fees and so on. As long as your costs are covered, you won't be putting any strain on your cash flow - and you shouldn't be able to get into too much trouble! In other words, you're setting things up so that there's a lot to gain - and not a lot to lose.

- Meanwhile, you need to let your investment 'rest' in order for it to grow. Over time, the value of the property (in particular, the land component) increases, and - since your debt stays the same - your equity also increases. Once you have a 10-15% increase in value, you can use the extra equity to 'fuel' the purchase of a second property - and so on, and so on, using exactly the same formula, and with no further claims on your income or other assets!

At the end of a 10 year period, you can have built up a portfolio of, say, 6 residential properties this way. If they've shown sufficient capital growth (and remember, house prices have doubled every 8-10 years this century) you need only sell one or two of them to reduce your borrowings on the whole portfolio. Which leaves you with strong equity in the remaining properties, plus the on-going rental income from them.

If all that seems too good to be true, I can tell you that it is possible: I'll be showing you how.

Case example: McDonalds

McDonalds Restaurants is one of my favourite examples of a system based on real estate.

When Ray Crock established the McDonalds franchise system in 1954-5, the menus consisted of only nine items, and the restaurants prided themselves on being able to sell and serve a 15-cent hamburger inside 60 seconds. By the end of the '50s, there were more than 80 restaurants across America, each franchise sold for around US$900: franchisees also paid Ray Crock a percentage of their investment as a franchise fee to cover administration. Unfortunately, huge business growth can't be sustained by limited capital - and therefore limited capital growth - and in the late '50s, McDonalds nearly collapsed under its own weight.

What saved McDonalds to grow into one of the outstanding businesses of the 20th century? Structured investment in real estate. *The company acquired all the restaurant properties and then* leased *them to the franchisees - retaining management of some restaurants themselves. In the following decades, this strong real estate base financed the building of thousands of restaurants all over the world. McDonalds is today worth billions of dollars because of a fundamental decision to restructure their cash flow, allowing them to acquire property, and to secure a steady demand for tenancy (through the success of the franchise), thus generating rental income. They started out with little or no equity.*

That's pretty much how our structure works: supplying property to willing tenants (within an affordable price range) to finance the building of a real estate portfolio for sustained capital growth.

HOW IT ALL WORKS: AN OVERVIEW

1: Gearing

You borrow 90% of the value of an investment property, giving you 10% equity. All it takes is 10% growth in the property's value - and you have 100% return on the capital you invested, per annum!

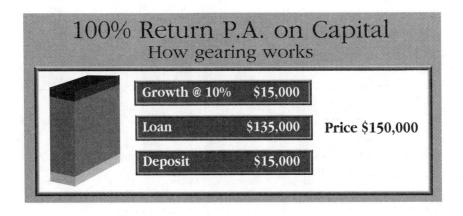

100% Return P.A. on Capital
How gearing works

Growth @ 10%	$15,000
Loan	$135,000	Price $150,000
Deposit	$15,000

Your 10% could represent a cash deposit, or you could use the equity in your own home, which may be more tax effective. (I'll deal with this in Chapter 7.)

2: Cash flow management

But what about the loan interest and all the other costs of doing this? Surely they eat away at your 100% return? No: that's where the structure comes in. It's all about *cash flow management* - the basis of all successful businesses.

3: Equity growth

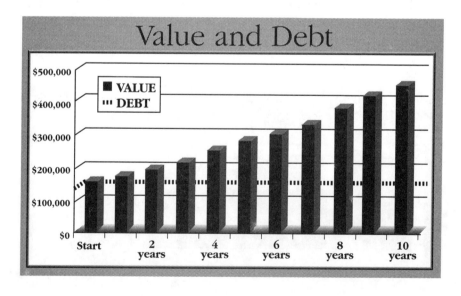

10-15% equity growth gives you the 10% equity you need to do the same again with your next property. And repeat. And repeat again.

If there's a warning bell ringing at the back of your mind about the *debt* you'll have chalked up by this time, don't worry: I promise to put that into perspective later on.

THE STARTING POINT

You can begin to build wealth now if you have:

- about $35,000 annual (combined gross) income
- and $20,000 in available equity (in your home or other property) or cash deposit (although there are ways of getting round this too...)

Don't forget, you needn't actually pay out any of your income. It's just an indicator of your ability to repay a loan: one of two criteria - equity being the other - on which banks and other institutions lend money for property investment. (In fact, you could actually *increase* your net income, thanks to tax savings, as we'll see in Chapter 6.)

THE GOAL

The following graph shows how the structure works, from the minimum starting point cited above.

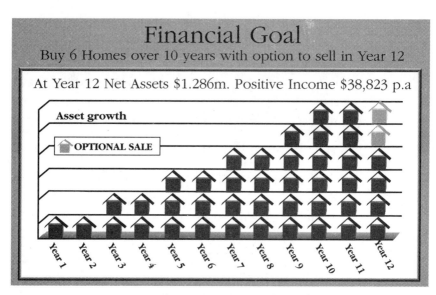

Financial Goal

Buy 6 Homes over 10 years with option to sell in Year 12

At Year 12 Net Assets $1.286m. Positive Income $38,823 p.a

Asset growth

OPTIONAL SALE

Year 1 Year 2 Year 3 Year 4 Year 5 Year 6 Year 7 Year 8 Year 9 Year 10 Year 11 Year 12

WHAT CAN YOU ACHIEVE?

Here's a slightly more aggressive use of the same structure.

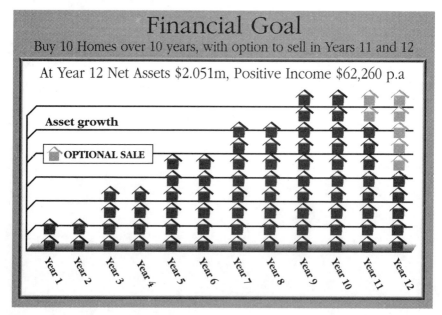

Financial Goal

Buy 10 Homes over 10 years, with option to sell in Years 11 and 12

At Year 12 Net Assets $2.051m, Positive Income $62,260 p.a

Asset growth

OPTIONAL SALE

Year 1 Year 2 Year 3 Year 4 Year 5 Year 6 Year 7 Year 8 Year 9 Year 10 Year 11 Year 12

I can't tell you what your commitment should be or what your potential is. It has to be up to you.

My best advice is: allow yourself to start small - and to think big.

WHAT DOES IT TAKE
TO MAKE THE STRUCTURE WORK?

We've already mentioned the key elements - but let's get specific. There are seven basic steps to building wealth.

1. Buy land for capital growth.

2. Optimise your income.

3. Maximise your tax benefits.

4. Finance to build.

5. Aim for affordability.

6. Make time work for you.

7. Be all you can be.

In Part B, I'll deal with each step in turn.

PART B
Seven steps
to wealth

Chapter 4 [Step 1]
Buy land for
capital growth

If you take away only one thing from this book, make this the one.

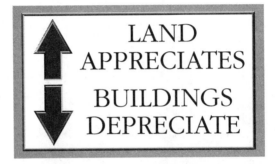

It's all to do with supply and demand. Land is a commodity which is obviously limited in supply, and for which demand is continually growing, as population increases. 'Bricks and mortar' are pegged to inflation and labour costs, so their price does go up - but they are not, as yet, in limited supply: buildings are pulled down (sometimes, before they fall down) and are easily replaced.

If you extract the land value from the growing value of house prices over a 30 - 40 year period, you can see that the land actually increases in value by nearly *twice* as much as the house value. As a compound effect, land in any 10 year period shows capital growth of around 15 - 20%, depending on location. The building component depreciates, effectively reducing the property's investment value - although inflation can camouflage the lack of capital growth. (During the '70s, just about everything went up in value by 10 - 15% per annum, but the lower inflation rates of the '90s have unmasked the real extent of growth.)

As an example, here's a graph showing the growth in house and land values in Mt Gravatt, a typical suburb of Brisbane.

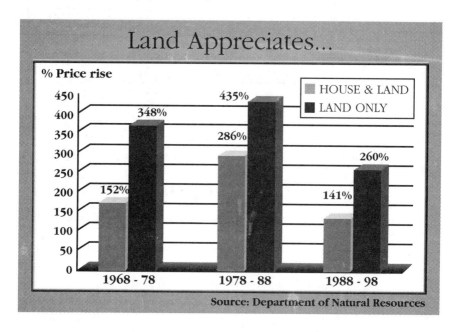

Unfortunately, if we are starting out with limited capital, we can't just buy land: we need a vehicle for generating income to service our debt. That vehicle is the *rental property*. But knowing that the land is the appreciating component, we need to acquire rental properties *with the highest possible proportion of land content.*

Take a look at this.

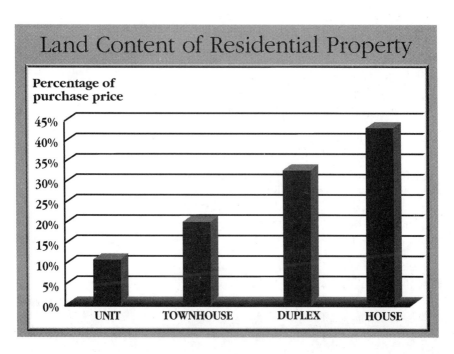

Land Content of Residential Property

Percentage of purchase price

45%
40%
35%
30%
25%
20%
15%
10%
5%
0%

UNIT   TOWNHOUSE   DUPLEX   HOUSE

In order to achieve real capital growth to allow you to build a portfolio over a 5-10 year period, you need to have *at least 30% land content.*

Duplexes and houses fall into the category of effective Wealth Building assets, with 30%+ land content. Townhouses within 7km of a CBD *can* also sneak into this bracket. (Check before you jump in.)

The 'good old' suburban home has the highest land content, and invariably gives the best capital growth.

BUT THEN - WHAT ABOUT UNITS?

I'll say it again: in order to achieve real capital growth over a 5 -10 year period, you need to have at least 30% land content. With most units and townhouses, you are lucky to find 10 - 15% land content within the purchase price.

Say you bought a residential unit as an investment over a 10 or 20 year period - as some 34% of investors do. The proportion of land value to building value is perhaps 10 : 90. Land appreciates, buildings depreciate - and you end up with limited capital growth (other than inflation) for the first five to ten years. This is *not* the way to start building a property portfolio...

Here is a comparison of house and highrise unit values in the last 10 years in the eastern seaboard capitals.

Most units have
very little land content

Forget the hype: one in five buyers are taking a loss on CBD units in Sydney and Melbourne, bought in the '90s. Why? Because only one in five of them buy to live in: the rest are speculators, who don't tend to look level-headedly at the real facts of supply and demand.

Yes, you will always find people who advise you to buy units. Don't buy land, they say: you'll incur land tax; tenants don't like mowing lawns; it's easier to find tenants for units than for houses.

Look behind the veil. The fact is that developers make a healthy profit from selling a number of units with nominal land value: is it any wonder they forget to mention that it's the *land* that appreciates?

As for land tax, it's there - but it's not nearly as bad as they make out. The unimproved land value has to exceed a set threshold (calculated differently from state to state) in each state. By the time you've reached the $160,000 per person threshold in Queensland, for example, you could be generating capital growth on three properties! And you only pay tax on the land value in excess of that amount.

A cautionary tale

Dainford Limited developed thousands of highrise units in their time, but they rarely held on to any, because they found that they tended to lose their value.

This came home to me during the early '80s, when units had dropped in value, and one of my associates went on a buying rampage. He clinically offered just 60-65% of the price that a unit had sold for less than three years previously, in nearly a dozen buildings across the Gold Coast. He held the units for ten years and sold them again, averaging a 13.5% per annum growth rate on his purchase price. He had the financial capacity to buy multiples of units and to make cash offers to desperate vendors.

In hindsight, he could have achieved the same kind of growth - without having to deal with desperate vendors, and without taking a huge cash outflow on the chin - simply by buying *houses at market value.* (He would have done even better, if

> **Developers make a healthy profit from selling a number of units with nominal land value: is it any wonder they forget to mention that it's the land that appreciates?**

he had bought *new* homes, and claimed the depreciation as a tax-deductible item, as discussed in Chapter 6.)

The real cautionary moral of the story, however, is the depreciating value of the units. My associate was able to buy them, second hand, at a capital *discount* of 30-40%. It is almost like buying that new BMW cabriolet (say) and driving it out of the showroom knowing that, as you cross over the grate, its value is probably dropping by 20-30%...

Case example

One of my favourite 'land appreciates, buildings depreciate' stories comes out of Queensland's Gold Coast. A guy bought the property (pictured below) in 1974 for $87,000 - and sold it in 1995 for $1.075 million. The house was a pull-down job, though rentable: the $1.075 million represented land value only!

DOES THE LOCATION MATTER?

Location is *vital* for capital growth.

I recently ran a Wealth Building workshop for a number of high-income individuals in Melbourne. At the start of the workshop, half of them affirmed that they were already investing to build wealth. I asked what their properties were, and where. Answer: they were units, in and around inner residential Melbourne. I asked what the land content of those units was. Answer: a sea of confused faces.

These people - competent, clued-up people - had acquired units in the area where they lived, purely on the basis that they would be easy to maintain and manage: a classic case of the 'I can drive by it on my way home from work' factor.

You *have* to do some homework - or find someone to do it for you.

Case example

A good friend of mine is the manager of a top hotel in Sydney: a very astute guy, who knows the intricacies of the hospitality business back to front. In 1994, he invested in the Canberra residential unit market, and acquired two townhouses there. When I asked him why, he said he did it for the tax benefits and to make some money. Wrong. His investment has actually showed him a loss to the point where the $60,000 capital he originally invested has all but been wiped out, and in 1997-98, there was no market for his units, due in part to the government's decentralisation policy: *there is currently a population exodus from Canberra, which will keep him in the abyss for perhaps another 3 - 5 years, or until policy changes.*

> You *have* to do some homework - or find someone to do it for you.

SO WHERE SHOULD YOU BUY FOR CAPITAL GROWTH?

The key factor is *demand*. And demand for residential property is underpinned by:

- population and
- employment.

The best-performing residential property investments are located in areas with the highest rate of growth in population and jobs, especially where there are still also affordable housing opportunities.

To give you some idea of the extent and distribution of population growth:

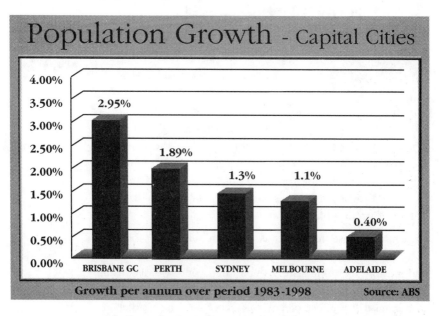

Population Growth - Capital Cities

Growth per annum over period 1983-1998   Source: ABS

You'll see that at the moment, Brisbane and Perth are showing the strongest population growth. This augurs well for long term growth in these markets. Melbourne and Adelaide will have to be watched carefully as downturns can hit hard.

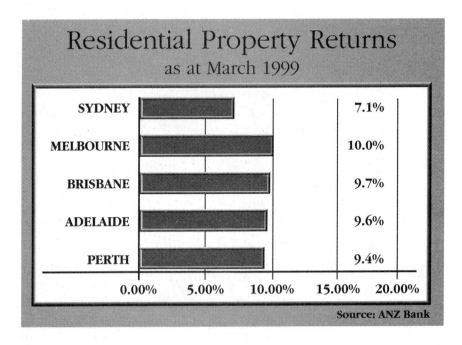

Residential Property Returns
as at March 1999

SYDNEY		7.1%
MELBOURNE		10.0%
BRISBANE		9.7%
ADELAIDE		9.6%
PERTH		9.4%

0.00%   5.00%   10.00%   15.00%   20.00%

Source: ANZ Bank

For the moment, this trend looks set to continue - particularly in Brisbane and the South-East Queensland Corridor. In 15 years' time, the area is predicted to overtake Melbourne as Australia's second largest city. Meanwhile, a number of major employers have announced their intention to relocate to Brisbane. These are the kind of factors to look out for, if you're going for capital growth.

Remember: 'close to home' is a rotten reason for buying property. In fact, there are advantages to buying out of state and in more than one state, as you build your portfolio. You can go where the growth is; you can spread your investment to minimise the effect of any fluctuations in the market in particular areas; and you can take advantage of the land tax excess threshold in each state.

Don't place too much emphasis on these broadbrushed median house prices. Remember it's the land that provides capital growth, not the buildings.

WHAT ABOUT REGIONAL AREAS?

The demand for property seems to be most consistent in capital cities.

I have had experience in the regional markets of Gladstone, Coffs Harbour, Cairns and even as close to a capital city as the Gold Coast. I have also witnessed, first hand, the problems experienced in Canberra and Newcastle when a dominant local employer decides to relocate.

In a capital city, you have a number of major industries feeding off each other, and a major population base which can attract new investment and further population growth.

Because we are talking about building up a portfolio, we could be in a position - in 10, 15 or 20 years' time - where we have accumulated 10 - 20 properties in a particular area. If a principal employer relocates or suffers financial strain (as with the government moving jobs out of Canberra, or BHP moving out of Newcastle), the area can free-fall into a downward spiral for anything up to ten years. Geelong, in Victoria, is another regional market that suffered badly during 1990-91, through the financial collapse of a major building society and the shut-down of manufacturing businesses: seven years later, the area hasn't yet bounced back, although the general property market in Melbourne has shown a solid recovery.

> Remember:
> 'close to home' is
> a rotten reason for
> buying property.

I live on the Gold Coast. I love the Gold Coast - yet for the next five years, I would probably class it as a regional market for the purposes of investment. In 15-20 years, forecasters believe the area will have merged with Brisbane, now an hour's drive away - and that's certainly something to keep an eye on for the future. But for the time being, the major industry on the Gold Coast is tourism, and its population is still under 400,000, of which a comparatively high percentage are welfare recipients.

Factors like the Asian currency crisis hit a tourism-based regional economy hard, driving unemployment up (in the case of the Gold Coast, from 9% to a forecast 14%). I wouldn't class the Gold Coast as an area for non-residents to build a portfolio in, until it reaches the 500,000 population mark and becomes a little bit more self-sustaining. On the other hand, its current volatility also makes it a highly dynamic market, with opportunities for people on the spot.

SUMMARY

LAND APPRECIATES, BUILDINGS DEPRECIATE

☑ Invest in a house/duplex with 30% land content.

PROPERTY APPRECIATES WITH DEMAND

☑ Invest where population and jobs are growing.

☑ Stay within 45 minutes' drive of a capital city.

And how do Australians currently invest in real estate?

*   ***34% BUY UNITS***
*   ***26% BUY WITHIN THEIR OWN POSTCODE***

No wonder most of us retire on welfare...

The beauty of getting this decision right, however, is that by buying in a growth area, you not only maximise the capital growth on your property: you also have a high tenant population from which to generate rental income! We'll talk about rent and renting, in Chapter 5.

Chapter 5
Optimise
your income

[Step 2]

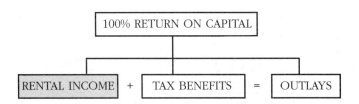

The beauty of gearing and leveraging your investment is that you can begin to build wealth with minimal capital, borrowing the balance of the acquisition costs of your first investment property. The downside is that you have to service that debt. And then there are other outlays, like maintenance and rates. The property doesn't pay for itself... Or does it? Residential property, as we've seen, has the potential to generate *income* to offset your cash outlays, while its capital value increases over time. Income is the fuel for capital growth.

For 'income', read 'RENT'.

WHO RENTS AND WHY?

95% of Australians have rented residential property at some time. More to the point, 30% of Australians *currently* rent residential property - and the number seems to be increasing.

There are increasing numbers of older people, empty nesters, dinks (double income, no kids) and single parent families in our population, and these categories tend to push up the demand for rental property. Another factor is that property price increases tend to outstrip inflation (which is great for capital growth) and therefore also outstrip rises in wages and salaries: the rental market grows, as property prices gradually rise beyond the reach of more and more people.

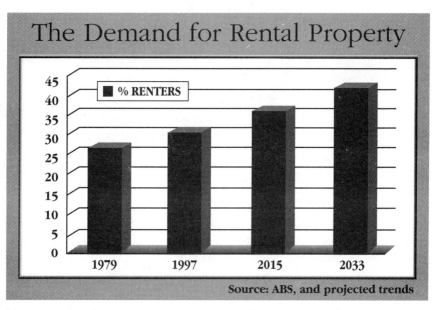

The Demand for Rental Property

■ % RENTERS

Source: ABS, and projected trends

At the same time, the number of occupants per property is dropping - partly in line with the ageing population.

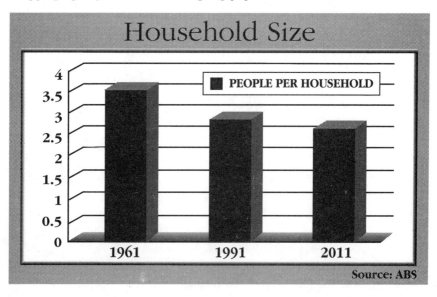

Household Size

■ PEOPLE PER HOUSEHOLD

Source: ABS

So we can safely project an increase in demand for rental property well into the 21st century.

There are many advantages to renting - although, of course, capital growth isn't one of them! Flexibility is a major factor, in view of increasing mobility and decreasing job security. Not having financial or managerial responsibility for a property is attractive to many people. And, as we noted in Chapter 1, a mortgage can seem like an unacceptable level of debt (if you don't look for the advantages of affordability, leverage and capital growth).

> We can safely project an increase in demand for rental property well into the 21st century.

One important thing to recognise, however, is that your market for tenants is principally made up of people in the lower income bracket. This is where the demand is. And to take advantage of that demand, we need to buy the kind of property that we can rent out at an affordable percentage of the average income. In other words: *aim for affordability* (Chapter 8). We'll come back to this a bit later, when we discuss the amount of rent we can charge.

OPTIMISING YOUR RENTAL INCOME

There are two ways you could theoretically go about optimising your rental income from a property.

- One is to maximise your income by charging the highest possible rent. If you charge the highest possible rent on the cheapest possible property, your margins look (in theory) particularly healthy.
- The other is to charge a moderate (even below-average) rent on a higher-priced property in a more popular residential area.

If you wanted to be greedy, you might think that the first option looked good - and you'd be shooting yourself in the foot.

Optimising rental income does not mean charging the *highest* rent: it means ensuring that the property attracts and retains tenants, and therefore maintains a *constant* rental income. The key is avoiding *vacancy,* which generates no income at all.

The two biggest factors in avoiding vacancy are:

- investing in an area with a high - and preferably growing - demand for rental property; and
- charging affordable, competitive rents.

Let's look at each of these in turn.

BEWARE 'BARGAINS'

We'll tackle the most common mistake first: it's a false economy to buy into a secondary suburb (high unemployment, low property values) because the property is 'cheap'. Property in a low-demand area may look like a bargain in pure purchase-price terms, but it won't show a return in consistent rental income. (In property, a 'bargain' is just a way for someone to unload their problems onto you...)

> In property,
> a 'bargain' is just
> a way for someone to
> unload their problems
> onto you...

We pinpointed Brisbane as a city currently showing significant population, employment and capital growth - and that's a step in the right direction - but you *still* need to do your homework. You could buy a house in some parts of Logan City, for example, for $80,000, and a unit for $60,000. If that sounds like 'good value', look again: double-digit unemployment figures, high youth crime rates - and, not surprisingly, a lot of vacant property! The area has tripped up a lot of property investors over the last 10 years. Developers and marketers have recklessly sold property which has been grossly overvalued, mainly to interstate buyers - who are now waking up to *negative* capital growth: in many cases, the real value of their property today might only be 60-70% of what they paid five years ago. And meanwhile, they have been struggling with low rental demand, and bearing the weekly cost of their borrowings. Cash flow nightmare...

This *doesn't* mean that rental property isn't a good investment. On the contrary - and despite a few urban myths - the rental market is growing steadily, and many people who rent do so through choice, even in the lower income brackets. What it *does* mean is that you need to do your homework on the location and type of rental property that will attract and retain consistent, rent-paying tenants!

WHERE DO RENTERS WANT TO LIVE?

According to the Urban Land Institute, there are six main reasons why people choose to live in a particular area.

1. Proximity to schools
2. Security (that is, safety) for the family
3. Adequate public transport
4. Proximity to shops
5. Availability of (or proximity to) employment
6. Recreational facilities

These reasons match my own survey findings in Brisbane. They don't seem to have changed at all over the last 30 years. In fact, they make pretty good sense - and are a useful guide to the kind of residential area that sustains a high demand for rental property.

Choose a property where at least the top three of these six factors are present within a radius of, say, 3 km: you'll not only be able to maintain a steady rental income, but capital growth as well.

Another factor is the *type* of property renters look for.

Even if you aren't thinking of resale values and capital growth, based on land content (as discussed in Chapter 4), you'd want to think twice about buying units for rental. If I remind you that only 6.1% of Australians owner-occupy units, you might be entitled to assume that everyone *rents* units. But the fact is that the *vacancy rate of units/townhouses is double that of houses in most areas:* in other words, more units lie empty and income-idle. Given affordability, that average Australian household of 2.8 people still prefers to live in detached housing.

Another tip: don't buy in *complexes* with multiple properties for sale to investors.

- You will be competing for tenants with all the other investor-landlords.

- Since owner-occupiers prefer areas with fewer rental properties, you will be limiting your property's sell-on potential - and hence your capital growth. Invest in areas with no more than 35% of homes occupied by renters. (Again, this weighs heavily against units, which are overwhelmingly renter-occupied.)

We've already mentioned, briefly, another good, practical yardstick for assessing the demand for rental property in a particular area: *vacancy factor.* Let's look at it in more detail.

VACANCY FACTOR

The rental vacancy factor is the percentage of the total rental properties in a particular area that are vacant at any given time. It is a pretty fair reflection of demand for rental property in that area - and therefore a barometer of how consistent your rental income will be.

The easiest and most accurate way of determining the vacancy factor in an area you are interested in is to contact a couple of the local real estate agents and simply ask them:

- how many rental properties they have on their books (in total); and
- how many of them are vacant at the moment.

Personally, I won't invest in an area where the rental vacancy factor is higher than 3%. This needs to be reassessed on a suburb by suburb basis as cities can vary from 1%-20%.

The following table shows the average rental vacancy factors across Australia, as compiled by the Real Estate Institute of Australia.

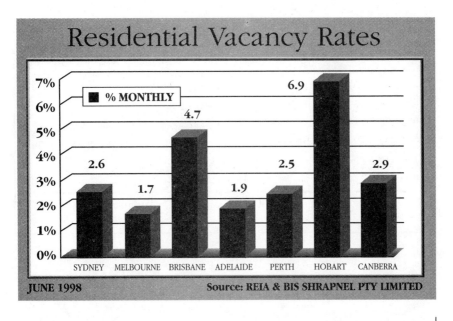

WHAT RENT SHOULD YOU CHARGE?

If your property is empty, it is income-idle. If you want to maintain a constant income, you need to secure a constant supply of tenants. One good way of doing this is to check the suitability and vacancy factor of an area before you buy. Another is to avoid being greedy about rent.

Buy rental property on which the market rate of rent is *no more than 30% of the average wage:* that makes it affordable to most people with a job. The average wage in 1999 is around $600 per week, so $180 per week is an affordable rent.

The following table shows average incomes in different states. I use it as a barometer for buying, and setting rent on, properties. It's one of those 'changeable weather patterns' I mentioned in the Introduction to this book, and requires on-going monitoring, as part of the basic discipline of Wealth Building.

Capital City Rental Affordability 1999					
	Sydney	Melbourne	Brisbane	Adelaide	Perth
Average Weekly Earnings	$640	$600	$584	$575	$576
Recommended Affordable Rental*	$192	$180	$175	$172	$173
*Based on 30% of average weekly ordinary time earnings. *Source: ABS 1999*					

Over the years, I have also made a point of renting my property around $10 *below* the going market rate. That way, if I advertise a house on Saturday, by Sunday afternoon I will have it rented to the tenant of my choice. At a cost of just $10 per week, I have avoided competition with most other rental properties advertised, ensured minimal vacant time, and had a number of applicants to choose from. Because I tend to acquire property at the low end of the range, my rents tend to be around $170 per week - which is highly affordable and attractive.

I see a lot of investors trying the opposite strategy, hanging out for the market rental value of their property, or more. For the sake of $5 or $10 per week, they might wait 4-6 weeks - during which the property is vacant - and in the end, settle for any tenant who comes along, increasing the risk of rapid tenant turnover - or worse. Even three weeks is a long period to have to pay the mortgage without the support of rental income.

> **Even three weeks is a long period to have to pay the mortgage without the support of rental income.**

The other temptation is for higher-income earners to buy expensive property and charge higher rents, thinking that - since they have more money - they should invest in a higher-priced property: it *must* be less hassle than two smaller properties. Not necessarily - and not the best way to build wealth. (We'll discuss this in more detail in Chapter 8.)

If your income is to pull its weight in offsetting your outlays, as our structure suggests, you will have to increase your rents from time to time in line with inflation. But if you have set a discounted rent in the first place, and if you have invested in an area with high and growing rental demand, this shouldn't be a problem.

Case example

In 1987 - 88, I acquired over 30 rental units in the regional town of Gladstone (south of Mackay), prior to commitment by Queensland government and industry to over a billion dollars in capital works projects in the area. I spoke to the real estate agent about the total number of properties he had under management: more than 400 at the time, including the ones I had acquired. And he hardly had a vacancy.

I couldn't understand why the rents were hovering at around $55 - $65 per week - and had been, for the best part of 6-7 years, in a high-inflation environment. The agent's answer was that he couldn't justify a rent increase - and when I told him I was proposing to increase my tenants' rent, he swore flat out that they simply wouldn't pay it. I went ahead and increased the average rent from $65 per week to $120 per week - and still did not have a single property vacant for more than two weeks at a time.

The moral of the story is: if you choose a high-demand, low-vacancy area, you will always have tenants, and you will be able to increase rents at least in line with inflation (or a percentage of the property's value) over the entire period of your ownership.

Post script: *I got out of Gladstone in 1989. Remember the vulnerability of regional markets (Chapter 4)? The promised investment in the city never came to fruition, and real estate prices have remained flat there for almost nine years... Chalk it up as one of my mistakes...*

RENTAL? BUT THAT MEANS TENANTS!

This is another one of those areas where emotion tends to overtake logic. We've all heard the horror stories of bikie gangs inhabiting a property, 10 people to a room, all but demolishing the house, never paying the rent, and leaving their luckless landlord with huge repair bills, a mortgage to service and eviction notices to draw up...

OK, there are 'problem' tenants. (In fact, mostly there are 'tenants with problems', which is not quite the same thing.) Some problems can be avoided, and others can be overcome.

☑ Set rents just below the market rate

This gives you greater discretion in choosing your tenants. It increases the likelihood that they will be able to continue to afford the rent. It also creates a degree of loyalty - and I find that tenants are more willing to look after the property and use their own initiative (and even money) to make small repairs and replacements, knowing that their landlord is helping them out a little.

At the end of the day, $10 per week off your bottom line income is a small price to pay for a comparatively hassle-free tenancy - particularly by the time you are the landlord of four or five properties...

☑ Check out prospective tenants the way you would a prospective employee

When the agents who manage my property tell me that they have a new tenant for it, I want to know:

* Has (s)he got a job, and how long has (s)he been at that job? Does the employer back this up?

$10 per week off you bottom line income is a small price
to pay for a comparatively hassle-free tenancy...

- Where has (s)he lived for the last five years? Did (s)he pay
  the rent? Was the bond refunded in full? Does the previous
  landlord back this up?

These two checks alone will weed out most potential bad
tenants. You really do need to know the answer to these
questions before you can rent a property - just like getting
references from somebody you might consider employing.
Potential good tenants won't mind being asked.

We've reproduced our Tenancy Application form at the end of
this chapter, if you're interested in the details.

✓ Cover the costs of the unexpected

People lose jobs, relationships break up, things happen.

Fortunately, there are insurance policies for almost everything, including some specifically tailored to rental properties. You can insure against financial loss - for example, by a tenant defaulting on rent or leaving without notice - if the outstanding amount is not already covered by the bond. You can insure the building and its contents against accidental damage, fire, theft, and malicious damage by the tenant. (The latter is actually pretty rare, despite the bikie gang stories!)

Do take out *Landlord Protection Insurance*. If you are buying a property for $150,000 - $200,000, on which the rent might be $175 per week, it will cost you around $500 per year (that's three weeks' rent) to take this insurance out. This will ensure that you will receive a full 52 weeks rent per year. In fact, we insist that all Custodian clients take out such insurance.

If a tenant leaves without paying the rent or causes malicious damage, the necessary bills can still be paid. It is absolutely vital to your Wealth Building program that you *maintain your cash flow:* you can't afford to be late with interest payments, because banks charge penalties - sometimes 3-4% above their going rate.

I also set aside a *contingency fund* of two months' rent, plus the amount of the excess payable on any insurance claim: that's usually enough to give everybody some leeway.

Case example

Some time ago, I rented a property to a nice young couple, both with jobs. They were in a de facto *relationship that had lasted for two years. Their jobs checked out, and the bond from their previous rental had been refunded in full. So far, so good. Unfortunately, the relationship hit the rocks, she moved out, he lost it, and then lost his job... Six weeks later (after I had evicted him), I found that he had used the ceiling in the third bedroom as an elaborate watering system for growing marijuana... The insurance covered $610. However, I had to fork out the money for repairs before the insurance company paid up - mainly so I could rent the property out again quickly: my policy didn't cover loss of rent. (In those days, I didn't worry about those things, but if I had had* then *the kind of policy I have* now, *the excess would only have been about $160... You live and learn.) As it was, the net cost to me was around $860 - about five weeks' rent.*

> If things can happen, they will - and usually all at the same time!

In light of this story, my formula of two months' rent plus rental insurance excess may seem overly cautious, but if you are building a portfolio of five or six properties, it's best to operate under Murphy's Law: if things can happen, they will - and usually all at the same time!

☑ Get someone else to take on the
   management tasks - and hassles - for you

A professional managing agent can take everything out of
your hands (if that's what you want): advertise the property;
vet and select tenants; organise maintenance; handle finance;
communicate with the tenants, local authorities and service
providers; and so on. (Over the page, I've reproduced the
form we use to ensure that agents vet our tenants effectively.)

Don't just give the property to *any* agent. As ever, look
behind the veil. Make sure the agent is well established:
a full-time Property Manager and a large rent roll with few
vacancies are good signs. Ask the agent for a reference from
some of his or her landlords. And please don't fall into the
trap of going with the agent who offers you the most
rent! Remember, higher rent can mean more hassles and
longer vacancies.

CONCLUSION

Don't let words like 'problem', 'insurance' and 'eviction' put
you off! Managing tenants is seldom as much of a hassle as
you might fear - even if you choose to handle it yourself.
And income from rent is the fuel for your capital growth.

Rental income on its own will not cover all your outlays on
an investment property. But there's another source of income
available from your investment property: paying less tax!
We'll go on to talk about tax benefits in Chapter 6.

Tenancy Application [Sample]

APPLICANT ONE

Full Name: _____ D.O.B. _____

Present Address: _____ Phone: _____

Period of Occupancy: _____

Reason for Leaving: _____

Name of Agent or Owner: _____ Rent Paid: _____

Address: _____ Phone: _____

Previous Address: _____

Period of Occupancy: _____

Reason for Leaving: _____

Name of Agent or Owner: _____ Rent Paid: _____

Address: _____ Phone: _____

Car Registration Number: ___ Drivers Licence No: ___ State: ___

Name of person to contact in case of emergency: _____

Address: _____ Phone: _____

PERSONAL REFERENCES (Not a relative)

1. Name: _____
    Address: _____ Phone: _____
    Relationship: _____ How long known: _____
2. Name: _____
    Address: _____ Phone: _____
    Relationship: _____ How long known: _____

IF STUDENT

Name of College, TAFE or University: _____

Faculty / Course: _____

Student ID Number: _____

Source: Peter Campbell Realty

OCCUPATION

Current Occupation: _____

Current Employer : _____

Address: _____

Phone: _____ Period of Employment: _____

Income: $_____

If employed for less than 6 months - previous employer: ___

If Self Employed - Industry: _____ How Long: _____

Accountant: _____ Phone: _____

Full Name of other persons (including children) wishing to occupy the above premises other than the Applicants: (Please include ages of children)

_____

Pets Owned: _____

Breed: _____

Are they registered with any Council: YES / NO

1. Have you ever been evicted by a Landlord or Agent?
    YES / NO   If yes, give details: _____
2. Have you been refused another property by any Landlord or Agent?
    YES / NO   If yes, give details: _____
3. Are you in debt to another Agent or Landlord?
    YES / NO   If yes, give details: _____
4. Is there any reason known to you that would effect your rental payments?
    YES / NO   If yes, give details: _____

DISCLAIMER / AUTHORITY

I, the said applicant, do solemnly and sincerely declare that the information contained in this application is true and correct and that all of the information was given of my own free will. I declare that I am not bankrupt. I further authorise the letting agent to contact and/or conduct any inquiries and/or searches with regard to the information and references supplied in this application.

I, the said applicant, do solemnly and sincerely declare:
I have inspected the property located at _____
I have of my own accord decided that I wish to rent the aforementioned property commencing _____ for a period of ___ months and that the rental on the property is $ _____ per week and the bond amount to be paid is $ _____ .
I have been informed, understand and agree that should this application not be accepted, the agent is not required to disclose why or supply any reason for the rejection of this application.

I have been informed, understand and agree that upon acceptance of this application, I will sign the appropriate paperwork and pay a minimum of one (1) week's rent within twenty four (24) hours of such acceptance. I have been informed, understand and agree that all monies are to be paid (being two (2) weeks' rent and bond) before commencement of the lease and collection of any keys to the property.

Privacy Act acknowledgement

In accordance with Section 18n (1) (b) of the Privacy Act, I authorise you to give information to and obtain information from all credit providers and references named in this application. I understand this can include information about my credit worthiness, credit standing, credit history or credit capacity. I understand this information may be used to assess my application.

Applicant one signature _____ Date _____

Applicant two signature _____ Date _____

NOTICE TO ALL
RESIDENTIAL TENANCY APPLICANTS

Before any application will be considered, each applicant must achieve a minimum of 100 check points.

Last 4 Rent Receipts	50 Points
Drivers License	40 Points
Passport	40 Points
Photo ID	30 Points
Pension Card	20 Points
Minimum 2 references from previous Landlord / Agent	20 Points
Pay Advice	15 Points
References	10 Points (each)
Current Motor Vehicle Rego Papers	10 Points
Copy of previous Telephone, Electricity or Gas Account	10 Points (each)
Bank Statement	10 Points
Copy of Birth Certificate	10 Points

Should you not be able to meet the 100 check points, please speak to the property manager.

Chapter 6
Maximise
your tax benefits

[Step 3]

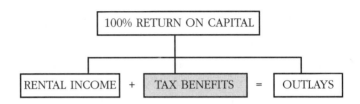

Alongside income, tax savings are the essential 'fuel' for building wealth.

It is fundamental to our structure that we maximise our tax benefits, thereby ensuring that we have minimal cash outlays on our investment property - thereby, in turn, placing no significant restrictions on our ability to build our portfolio by re-investing our increased equity.

This - at last! - is where 'negative gearing' comes in.

WHAT IS NEGATIVE GEARING?

Gearing is borrowing money for the purposes of investment - and we will be discussing how to get the most out of it in Chapter 7, on obtaining and using finance.

Negative gearing is the tax benefit that accrues when the income from an investment fails to cover the outlays on that investment, so that you are making a 'book loss', or negative income. (Don't panic: remember, the capital value of your asset is still growing...) A residential investment property would be negatively-geared if, for example, the mortgage payments and other tax-deductible items exceeded the rental income.

Definition

Negative gearing occurs when your total outlays to maintain an investment are greater than your income from the investment: the difference is claimable as a tax deduction.

The thing is, this loss - the difference between your outlays and your income - is *tax deductible*. It can be offset against your personal income (including salary) to reduce your taxable income, and perhaps even put you into a lower tax bracket. The upshot is that you *pay less tax* - and if that doesn't sound like a good idea, there's something pretty unusual about your thinking...

WHAT DEDUCTIONS CAN YOU CLAIM?

Here are some of the main cash deductions you can claim on any rental property.

- ☑ Loan interest. (Other borrowing costs - loan application and valuation fees, mortgage registration and insurance etc - are non-cash or 'paper' deductions)
- ☑ Insurance premiums
- ☑ Fees - for example, for property/rental management, legal advice and accountancy (if you decide to get all these deductions drawn up by a professional. You could also pay your spouse a fee for keeping regular accounts on the property, and claim that!)
- ☑ Rates and local government charges
- ☑ Maintenance, repair and upkeep costs
- ☑ Sundry business expenses - like bank charges, stationery and travel (including reasonable inspections of property out of state)

Here's an example. Say you purchase a rental property for $150,000, borrowing 90% of the purchase price at 7% interest only, and you let it out at $180 per week for 50 weeks of the year, for an annual rental income of $9,000.

		Rental income	$9,000
Deductions:	$		
Loan interest	9,450		
Insurance	130		
Maintenance	508		
Rates	1,000		
Rental management	702		
TOTAL CASH OUTLAYS	11,790		
Borrowing costs	400		
TOTAL DEDUCTIONS	($12,190)		
Shortfall			($3,190)

That shortfall is deducted from your gross income - say, $45,000, to give you a taxable income of $41,810. Here's the basic calculation:

		After deductions on property:	
Gross income:	$45,000	Taxable income:	$41,810
Tax payable:	$11,952	Tax payable:	$10,580
Net after-tax		Net after-tax	
income:	$33,048	income:	$34,420
		Tax refund:	$1,372

This example was based on your buying an older property - as 77% of investors who take advantage of negative gearing do. It doesn't offer much of a tax deduction, but it is a negatively geared asset, so you do get a tax saving.

THE DIFFERENCE THAT MAKES
A DIFFERENCE: DEPRECIATION

The *depreciation of an asset used to produce income* is a non-cash deductible item. This means you can claim a percentage of the declining value of furniture, fixtures and fittings, over a number of years of wear and tear. But somewhere in that list of depreciating items - carpets, curtains, cupboards, cookers - is the biggest item of all: the building.

Here's the key: a residential building constructed after July 1985 that is used to produce income can be depreciated.

Construction commenced:	Claimable depreciation rate:	Over:
July 1985 - September 1987	4%	25 years
September 1987 onwards	2.5%	40 years

Depreciation on a new building can add up to thousands of dollars a year - and it's a 'non-cash' deduction, which means that you don't actually have to lay out any cash each year in order to claim the 'loss'! This is the factor that significantly reduces your taxable income - and your tax payments. It's what makes our *income + tax benefits = outlays* structure work best.

Let's look at our example, supposing now that you bought a *new* rental property of the same value and on the same terms.

		Rental income	$9,000
	$		
TOTAL CASH OUTLAYS	11,790		
NON-CASH COSTS			
Borrowing costs	400		
Depreciation	8,149		
TOTAL DEDUCTIONS	($20,339)		
Shortfall			($11,339)

Your taxable income is now ($45,000 - $11,339) = $33,661.

And here's the new refund calculation:

After deductions on new property:

Gross income:	$45,000	Taxable income:	$33,661
Tax payable:	$11,952	Tax payable:	$ 7,467
Net after-tax		Net after-tax	
income:	$33,048	income:	$37,533

You have effectively increased your net income by **$4,485.**
And think of it purely in cashflow terms:

INVESTMENT CASH FLOW

	$	
Rental income	9,000	per annum
Cash outlays	(11,790)	per annum
Cash shortfall	(2,790)	per annum
Tax rebate (after non-cash deductions)	4,485	per annum
After tax cost	NIL	
Cash refund	$1,695	per annum

This allows you an earlier opportunity to add onto your portfolio without eating into your personal cashflow. And our example only shows one property: multiply the effect by five or six...

It's all about *cashflow management.* You've got the opportunity to write off the entire value of the house and fittings over the years, leaving only the bare land value - which is the part of your investment that's going to go up in value. The components of your house and land package should add up something like this:

Total purchase price		$200,000
Land	$80,000	
House (structure)	$100,000	
Fittings	$20,000	

You can write off the fittings over the first five years, which is a major boost to your income, and to your ability to add on to your portfolio during that period. That's efficient cash flow management, and efficient Wealth Building.

WHO WANTS TO PAY MORE TAX THAN THEY HAVE TO?

I know the maths can be a bit mind boggling - but it's not essential to do all the sums at this stage. (Once you get into negatively-geared investments, it's a good idea, in any case, to have your tax return completed by a competent accountant or tax adviser, so that you are sure to claim all your legitimate deductions.)

But here's the bottom line. Am I really saying that by claiming a book 'loss', you can not only cover the shortfall - but actually walk away with extra cash in your pay packet? That's exactly what I'm saying.

At the moment, if you are on a salary of $68,000, you may have to work Monday and Tuesday of each week *just to pay the tax!*

> Am I saying that you can actually walk away with extra cash in your pay packet? That's exactly what I'm saying.

Negative gearing allows you legitimately to minimise the amount of tax you pay - as well as fueling capital growth. Negatively-geared rental property is one of the most tax-efficient investment vehicles available.

Some people think about buying older properties for investment purposes

If you are a PAYE tax payer, and your deductions are more than $500 for the year, you don't even have to wait for an end-of-year refund: you can claim an immediate adjustment to the tax that is deducted from your salary at source by your employer. (Section 221 D of the Tax Act provides for this PAYE adjustment - and the form used to claim for it is called the 221D Form.)

Anybody on PAYE ought to look into this! The higher your income - and your marginal tax rate - the more tax you can save.

AND HOW *DO* AUSTRALIANS INVEST?

Let's complete the grim picture.
* ***34% BUY UNITS***
* ***26% BUY IN THEIR OWN POSTCODE, and***
* ***ONLY 3% MAXIMISE THEIR TAX BENEFITS WITH OPTIMUM CAPITAL GROWTH!***

NEED ANY FURTHER INCENTIVES?

There are a couple of other little gems hidden in the fine print of the Tax Act, which can also improve your bottom line.

- Under Section 51(1), you can pay 10% of the total rental income to your spouse, a friend, or other nominated person, as a fee for managing the books of your rental property. (We call this 'grocery money'.)

- Another 'perk' in owning properties interstate is that you can travel to see them twice a year (and take your book-keeper) - and deduct the full cost of the travel, as well as one night's accommodation, while you inspect your property and meet with the agent. (This is something we'd encourage you to do anyway - but why not stay for a few extra days and make a break of it?)

POSITIVE THINKING FOR NEGATIVE GEARING

> This isn't your home we're talking about, it's a negatively-geared asset.

Quite bluntly, if you buy a house built before 1985 as an investment property, you need your head read! Why would you do it?

A lot of investors acquire older properties, because they think they are 'better value' (they can save an extra $5,000 or $10,000 on the purchase price) and of course they 'prefer the feel' of an older house. But - at the risk of repeating myself - it is the *land* that appreciates in value: the house is only the vehicle by which we can generate rental income and qualify for tax deductions, so that we can cover our outlays while we achieve capital growth.

It really doesn't matter if we pay a little bit extra for a newer property: it will more than pay for itself via a substantial tax rebate. And sorry, but it *really* doesn't matter if you 'like' an old house: this isn't your home we're talking about, it's a negatively-geared asset to offset your tax and maximise your income. Logic - not emotion - for capital growth.

Remember our structure: that's what cash flow management and negative gearing are all about. Using the figures from our example on page 99:

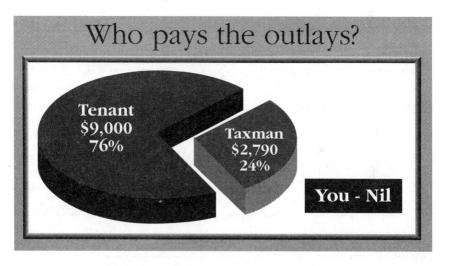

Who pays the outlays?

Tenant
$9,000
76%

Taxman
$2,790
24%

You - Nil

Case example

Here is a comparison of two styles of investment in residential property. The first is that of an investor we might call Enthusiastic But Misguided, who has snapped up Old Mrs Reid's House round the corner. The second is a real-life investor from North Queensland, whom we can (rightly) call the Wealth Builder.

	Enthusiastic But... (1 older property)	Wealth Builder (3 new properties)
Property value	$300,000	$365,000
Equity	$100,000	$60,000
Borrowed	$200,000	$305,000
Income per week	$300	$435
Outlays per week		
Loan payments	(P & I) $335	(Interest only) $410
Other costs	(Maintenance) $40	(Costs,charges) $120
	(Rates/land tax) $40	
	$415	$530
Net cash shortfall	$115	$95
Depreciation	NIL	$300
Tax rebate 44% (excl. principle repayments)	$22	$182
NET CASH per week	($93)	$87
Capital growth over 5 years	$101,000 (6%)	$253,000 (10%)

As you can see, the Wealth Builder has used 60% of the equity to achieve more than double the growth, with a cash positive position of $87 per week. The Enthusiastic But Misguided investor who purchased Old Mrs Reid's house, on the other hand, finds that it is costing him $93 per week, and double the equity, to get half the growth over a five year period. The Wealth Builder will have increased his portfolio value by five to six times that of Enthusiastic over a ten year period, using the same equity base...

Food for thought?

Chapter 7
Finance
to build

[Step 4]

In Chapter 3, we saw that building a portfolio is based on gearing, and the way it can be leveraged when you buy residential real estate, so that you can:

- minimise your initial capital input into the investment (10% equity) and
- use the bank's money - in effect - to build wealth (90% borrowing) by
- reaping 100% per annum return on your capital, while
- offsetting your costs with rental income and the tax benefits of negative gearing and
- using equity growth to provide start-up equity for subsequent acquisitions.

I trust that, by now, all that sounds pretty straight forward! (If it doesn't: don't worry. Really. As you investigate further, and still more as you begin to work the system, it will all fall into place as far as it needs to.)

In this chapter, we look at some of the practical issues around gearing: property values and valuations, choosing and using loan providers, and evaluating different finance options.

ASSESSING THE VALUE OF YOUR PROPERTY

It's vital for you to be able to make a basic assessment of the value of a property, so that you can check that you are paying a fair price.

The key to the valuation - and capital growth - of your property will (as ever) be the land.

One simple method of determining the value of your investment is to divide it into two components: the land value, and the replacement cost of the building.

For a house, this is quite simple: you can usually estimate the *land value* by sales of comparable vacant land sites. This information can be obtained from the Department of Valuer Generals or the Department of Natural Resources: you just have to request a sale report of all residential allotments within a recent period. (Alternatively, *rates notices* include 'unimproved land values'.) Another easy method is to ask the real estate agent or developer about the land component of a property. In a new estate, this is pretty straightforward, and you should also get some forecasts of future development and projected land values, as an indication of how your equity might increase over time.

The other component is the *replacement cost* of the house. You can estimate this by a simple formula:

Total size of house (square metres) x $ rate per square metre

Builders aren't always eager to give out rates per metre, but in most capital cities you can find project homes advertised in the newspapers, with a reasonable range of standard building rates - from $600 to $800 per square metre. This doesn't include footings, so add on another $30 per square metre for footings and earthworks, and then have a quantity surveyor identify the value of your fixtures and fittings, as well as landscaping. (In any case, it's a good idea to get a quantity surveyor's valuation when you are claiming tax deductions for depreciation, as discussed in chapter 6 - and for $200 or $300, this is a useful cross-check.)

The other method of assessing a property's value is simply looking at *comparable sales*. However, this is an inaccurate approach at best, and can be deceptive. You don't know the circumstances of the purchaser or vendor, which may have distorted the price. In the case of blocks of units, they may have been sold with incentives, or to non-resident owners who didn't bother to check out the value beneath the price tag - with the result that few owners have actually paid anything resembling replacement cost. I prefer to do a search with the Department of Natural Resources (in Queensland, or the Valuer General in other states), checking sales over the previous six months where the purchaser's address coincides with the property sold: that is, where the owner is a resident.

BANK VALUATIONS

The dynamic of equity growth (using interest-only loans) is that the debt stays constant, while the value of the property goes up. But who defines the 'value' part of that equation? For the purposes of assessing equity, the only valuation that matters is the one adopted by the bank that is lending you the balance of the acquisition costs.

> **Bank valuations can be deceptive - and potentially disastrous.**

Ideally, the value used by your lender should be the same as the purchase price, or more.

If the bank valuation is significantly lower than the purchase price (and therefore the amount of the loan), the bank may protect itself by writing down the security value of the property - and this can affect your total equity position with that bank. Unfortunately, this is not a rare occurrence: bank valuations can be deceptive - and potentially disastrous.

Let's say your home is worth $250,000, and you have a debt with the bank of $100,000.

You apply to buy a new investment property, priced at $180,000: you decide to use the equity from your home, and roll the loans together into a single loan package, which allows you to borrow 100% of the purchase price, plus costs. (This is called *zero-cost financing*, which we'll discuss further, a bit later in the chapter.) However, the bank's valuation of your investment property - undisclosed to you - is only $150,000. Here's what happens.

Own home:	House value	$250,000
	Borrowed	$100,000
	Equity	$150,000
		(60%)
Investment property:	Purchase price	$180,000
	Costs	$20,000
	Borrow	$200,000
	Bank valuation	$150,000

Total security value of assets (house value + bank's valuation of investment property):		$400,000
Total borrowings:		$300,000
	Equity:	$100,000
		(25%)

Your equity has plunged from 60% to 25%, and your net assets from $150,000 to $100,000 - according to the bank. And you're not unique: this happens depressingly often. People purchase all types of investment property - from high-rise units to town house units and houses - at over-inflated prices: anything from $30,000 to $100,000 over the bank's appraisal of the property's security value.

Frankly, I think it's outrageous that banks continue to do this sort of thing. If they aren't prepared to disclose their valuer's appraisal of the security value of the investment property, their loan should be limited to the amount of their valuation. It could take investors 5 - 10 years to recoup their lost capital as a result of a wide differential! At the time of writing, the Commonwealth Bank does have a policy to disclose any differential in valuation greater than 10% - but other major banks don't.

Caveat emptor: buyer, beware. To ensure you don't get caught out on this, consider:

* taking out a separate loan for your investment property
* with a different bank to the one that has your home loan.

This also gives you added protection, should there be a problem with your investment portfolio at any time, since your home isn't tied up with your investment.

You can still use the equity in your own home effectively, by simply applying to your home loan bank for the 10% deposit on your first investment property.

In any case, find a lender who is prepared to disclose the security value of the property you are acquiring. If you are acquiring it through an agent and using a finance broker, obtain a copy of the valuation. Ensure that it equals your purchase price or comes within, say, 5% of it. (I must admit that I have often had to settle for an assessment that didn't quite meet my price. Read on, and you'll know why...)

VALUERS

Given that it is the bank's perception of the value of the property that matters, you'd hope to be able to have confidence in the people they get to do the valuations. Nice idea.

Banks will often instruct panel valuers to value the property - and some of the most frustrating experiences I've had in real estate investment over the years have been dealings with these self-styled 'experts' in property. Valuations are not, at the best of times, an exact science. The banks use valuers because they have an insurance indemnity: if an investor defaults, and it is found that the property valuation was not representative of market values at the time of purchase, the bank can claim against the valuer.

I, personally, have seen the same property valued by three different valuers, where the highest valuation was double the lowest!

> Given that it is the bank's perception of the value of the property that matters, you'd hope to be able to have confidence in the people they get to do the valuations. Nice idea.

The big valuation firms tend to have young valuers, in their twenties, doing 10-15 valuations a day - which doesn't make for the most painstaking research. They will search an area, through the Valuer General's Department, and find a benchmark, or range of sales. The Valuer General's sales records are three to six months old, so if the market is really moving, it may not be reflected by the valuation. Moreover, the valuers will often use the *lowest* comparable sale price for your purchase - because their instructions from the bank are to supply a value at which the property would sell in the local market within three months. (This may vary if you have been required to take out mortgage insurance.)

Valuers will quite openly admit that if they were valuing a property for *you* - as opposed to the bank - they might strike a higher valuation figure. As it is, they are bound to be conservative.

So the valuation may well be a little under your price - but anything over 5% is a worry. Don't forget: this is the basis of the bank's assessment of your net equity!

Once again: do the homework. (Preferably, yourself.) Find comparable sales *to locals* - not out-of-state speculators - and if you can't: *don't buy.*

The point is: don't expect too much from valuers - but remember that the banks will rely on them. You need to work with them in order to secure equity growth and build a property portfolio. It's a good idea to:

- establish a relationship with the bank-appointed valuer yourself, so you understand his or her methodology in carrying out the initial valuation of a property. Don't be afraid to argue the point. (As I mentioned above, most busy valuers are *so* busy that they tend to be conservative - but I've also seen them accept good, up-to-date evidence and change their initial appraisal.);

- ask that valuer to revisit your property, once you become aware that there may have been some increase in values, and on a six- to twelve-month basis. This way, you have access to the valuation information - and you know that this valuer's appraisal will be accepted by the bank.

If you are going to appoint your own valuers, check that they will be acceptable to your bank.

CHOOSING A LOAN PROVIDER

Selecting the right source of finance for your investment portfolio will be integral to your capacity to build wealth.

This is another one of those decisions that needs to be made on logic, not emotion. Don't get sentimental about banks. Don't feel you have to be loyal to a bank - even if it's a big name, it sponsors your favourite sporting event, it already holds your account or home loan, and the staff are friendly at your local branch! With banks, loyalty only goes one way: they are uncaring at best - and at worst, they can be incompetent or manipulative, or both.

Remember our muscle-building analogy in Chapter 3? If finance corresponds to the carbohydrates that fuel your exercise, the lender is merely the brand of cereal or bread you choose to provide those carbohydrates. If you don't like the flavour of one - switch to another. Fortunately, competition is

> Don't get sentimental about banks.

increasing within - and from outside - the bank sector, and you should be able to find a lender willing to accommodate you, if you shop around.

So what is a logical way of selecting and dealing with a loan provider? Here are a few of the major considerations.

- You need to establish with the bank from the outset that you intend to use the increased equity on the property to build an investment portfolio. Most of the important questions and decisions flow from there.

- Banks lend against *security*. You need to know the bank's loan-to-valuation ratio (LVR) - what percentage it will lend on investment property. Some banks only lend 60% of

valuation (or contract price), and others 90%. You are
looking for a bank that will accept a 10% equity position.
Because, under our structure, all your outlays are being
met, you can afford to borrow 90% - and then, as soon as
your first property increases in value by 10%, you should
have enough equity with that bank to acquire a second
property (and so on). If a bank requires 20% equity, it will
take you twice as long to build a portfolio - with that
particular bank.

Also, be aware that over time, the bank may move the
goal posts on their lending criteria. This may be your
signal to change banks...

For a loan of over 80%, you will be required to take out
mortgage insurance, to cover the lender against potential
losses if you default. (This is a once-only payment - and

This may be a signal to change your lender

tax deductible.) The main insurers - HLIC or MGICA - may call for an independent valuation, so it is a good idea to ensure that the bank's valuer is on the mortgage valuation panel as well.

- Banks also lend against your anticipated ability to service the debt: that is, to maintain repayments. The *affordability* of the loan is calculated by total repayments (of all loans, credit card debts and so on) as a percentage of your gross income. Most banks are comfortable with 30% - 35%, but the figure can go as low as 25% and as high as 60%: shop around.

  Ensure that at least 80% of the projected rental income from the investment property is included in your income for credit assessment, and that the tax savings on negative gearing are taken into account: different banks calculate this in different ways, and it can make a big difference to how much you can borrow.

- The bank must be prepared to *disclose its appraisal of the security value* of the property, for comparison with the purchase price.

- Check for unnecessary or hidden *fees:* loan application fees, valuation fees, penalties for paying out (including refinancing) early, administration charges and so on.

- The bank must be flexible about *revisiting valuations.* Property, roughly speaking, doubles in value every 8 - 10 years, but within that trend there are constant fluctuations: you need to be checking comparable sales for signs of rising values - and the increased equity that you can use to increase your portfolio. Some of the major banks are less inclined to consider a revised valuation within 12 months of acquisition.

I have compiled a table of investment banks, what they will lend, and options for building a portfolio.

Major Financial Institutions' Lending Guidelines

Lender	Application Fee	Mortgage Ins. Fee	% Lent on Valuation	% Rent Applied	Valuation Disclosed	Revalue at 12 months
Westpac	$750	1.9% Loan	90	75	No	Yes
Commonwealth	$450-$600	1.9% Loan	90	80	>10%	Yes
ANZ	$400-$600	1.9% Loan	90	60	No	Yes
NAB	$400	1.9% Loan	90	80	No	Yes
Metway	$550	1.9% Loan	90	80	No	Yes
Aussie Home Loans	$600	1.9% Loan	90	80	No	Yes
Bank of Melb.	$250-$750	1.9% Loan	90	80	No	Yes
St. George	$500	1.9% Loan	90	80	No	Yes
RAMS	$595	1.9% Loan	90	80	No	Yes

Source: Access Finance

As you can see, none of the banks disclose valuations, or revisit valuations inside of 12 months, and the ANZ will only take 60% of your rental income into account. You will need to monitor such policies, and push for their relaxation, if you are going to make the structure work - but you will find more flexibility among second-tier banks than among the Big Four.

Loans are also available from some of the major insurance companies and credit unions, or through a mortgage broker (for a fee), but frankly, it is the second-tier banks that are going to be most useful to you in building your property portfolio. Again, shop around. It may be worth paying an extra 0.25% - 0.50% in interest rates to find a lender who is prepared to support you in building a portfolio over time. Be prepared to negotiate the interest rate. Indicate your intentions and ask questions. You might be able to obtain pre-approval at the time of your first acquisition.

Using a broker

There are some big advantages in using a Finance Broker to shop around for a deal for you. If you go to a major broker, they can often get you a better deal with your own bank than you could get by going direct to your bank manager. (Sad, isn't it?) Some of these brokers are doing $100 - $200 million worth of financing per month - and the banks are happy to pay them commissions and trail fees (a percentage of your interest for the life of the loan) in order to secure the business.

> A major broker can often get you a better deal with your own bank than you could. (Sad, isn't it?)

Your first port of call might naturally have been your local bank manager (who after all has probably been knocking on your door, wanting to lend you money). But if you are using your home as part of the equity, it could be harder than pulling sharks' teeth to get your home mortgage released from your investment portfolio (which has got to be your short-term goal). Local bank managers tend not to like this idea, because their security is better served by holding the deed to your home - but a broker has the negotiating power to represent *your* interests.

Some of the smaller brokers charge a fee for their service, but if you are going to use a broker, I would in any case recommend one of the larger ones, who have got the turnover - and therefore the negotiating power - to get you the best deal. Test them out and get them to offer you financing through a couple of banks on the terms and conditions you want - including having the valuation disclosed *and* the option to use equity in six to twelve months to repurchase.

CHOOSING A FINANCE OPTION

Zero-cost financing

This is really just a fancy term for using the equity in your own home as collateral security for your investment property, instead of having to find a cash deposit. (We gave one example of how this could be done, earlier, emphasising that the bank's valuation must be the same as the purchase price.) This can be highly tax effective, as all your costs of acquiring the *investment* property, and the interest costs of the loan, can be deducted from your income tax. The repayments on your *home* are not similarly tax deductible. So if you do have spare cash, you are far better off using it to pay off your existing home mortgage, rolling the loans together, and, in effect, borrowing 100-110% on your investment property! Let's look at some numbers.

Home value	$200,000
Outstanding debt	$100,000
Value of investment property	$150,000
Stamp duty, legal/finance costs etc	$ 9,500
Total acquisition costs	$159,500
Total assets (bank's valuation)	$350,000
Total debt	$259,500
Of which:	
Investment debt (tax deductible)	$159,500

Your goal should be to try and divert as much of your taxable income into your Wealth Building program a possible - using all legal opportunities available to you - in order to minimise your tax.

Interest only loans

Maximum tax deductions are based on interest only loans, as opposed to Principal and Interest (P & I) loans, because only *interest* payments are tax deductible.

Banks aren't always enthusiastic about this, as they prefer some principal to be paid off, but as you've probably gathered, by now, Wealth Building is about *managing your cash flow:* where you have an opportunity to minimise your cash outlays, do it. This will allow you to build earlier. (If you have any spare cash, use it to pay off the principal on your home loan.)

If you took a P & I loan for $150,000 over 25 years, in the first five years you would repay $13,257, or about 9% of the loan. This would affect your cash flow by $51 per week (in after tax dollars). It's also money that could otherwise have been ploughed back into Wealth Building.

Locking in a rate of interest

The most important thing in Wealth Building (if I may say it just one more time) is to manage our cash flow - not to get the highest rent, *nor the lowest interest rate.* My advice is to lock in your loan at the best rate you can find, for as long as you can.

You don't have to be in the business of interest rate forecasting to do this - although there are hundreds of economists and pseudo-economists who will offer you the crystal ball. If interest rates are at 7% and you can lock in for five years, do it: it's not going to be of tremendous consequence if they fall to 6%. You were happy with 7%: live with it.

As a worst case scenario, if you are locked in at 7% for five years, you could come out of the lock-in period with interest rates at 14%. But as interest rates increase, so do rents, and so too do the values of properties. (Surprisingly, demand also seems to remain high. In 1988-89, for example, interest rates went as high as 17% and there was a market frenzy such as I'd never seen.)

GEARING IN ACTION

Under our structure, you use the equity in your house, or put forward a cash deposit, for 10% of the purchase price of a new residential investment property which - thanks to rental income and negative gearing - thereafter pays for itself. When the value of the property has increased by 10%, you should have enough equity with the bank that loaned you the balance (assuming it is prepared to maintain a 10% equity position) to acquire a second investment property. You now have two assets working for you, both increasing in value and enabling you - in a shorter period of time - to build up further equity, to acquire your third property... And so on.

Once you've acquired your second property, you are already in the charmed realm of the top individual investors.

- 87% acquire only one property
- 13% acquire more than one property
- Less than 1.5% acquire more than four properties

There will obviously be a limit to how many properties you can acquire over a given period of time - depending on your income, the rate of equity growth, and the amount of money your investment bank is prepared to lend you to build a portfolio. Discuss these things with a few prospective lenders. Remember, you can start small - and think big. It's not a race. Finance to build.

Chapter 8

Aim for

affordability

[Step 5]

As I travel around Australia talking about Wealth Building and residential real estate, I find that almost everybody is prepared to get excited about land appreciating (for capital growth) and buildings depreciating (for negative gearing), about maximising income and reducing tax. There are always a few doubts, concerns and 'what if?' questions (which I address in Chapter 11), but there's only one really big 'Yes But...' And that's the dreaded Real Estate Cycle.

Booms and busts. Upturns and downturns. Height of the market, depth of the recession. What happens if you buy or sell at the wrong time or at the wrong price?

Let's get some perspective about this.

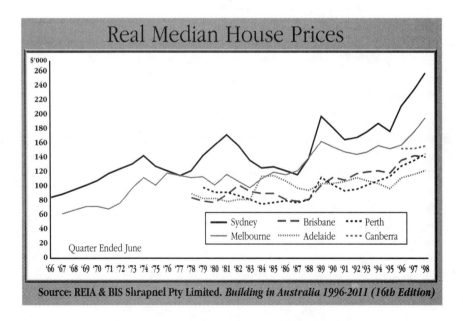

Real Median House Prices

Quarter Ended June

Legend: Sydney — Brisbane — — Perth · · · · Melbourne ·········· Adelaide ········· Canberra - - - -

Source: REIA & BIS Shrapnel Pty Limited. *Building in Australia 1996-2011 (16th Edition)*

UPS AND DOWNS

The idea of economic cycles is practically synonymous with real estate investment. And as usual, everyone remotely connected with the industry - and his dog - has got a well-established theory about where we are in the cycle at any given time. If you talk about the history of cycles, and booms and busts, someone will always try to maintain that 'it won't happen again' - until it happens again... The bad news is that downturns do happen. The good news is that the upswings invariably follow - and that it is never 'too late' to find real opportunities for capital growth.

> Someone will always try to maintain that 'it won't happen again' - until it happens again...

When I was at school, I used to work in my father's menswear shop in Belgrave (in country Victoria) during the holidays. I'd often start work at 8.30am, and not see a single customer until 11.00am - and then, quite suddenly, four or five unrelated customers would walk in at the same time. You'd expect the same to happen at lunchtime, but then it would be quiet until some random point in the afternoon, when I'd be rushed off my feet all over again.

If you ever wait for trains or buses, you may recognise the same phenomenon. There is no obvious rhyme or reason to the frenzies of activity, and inactivity - despite the timetable! In real estate terms, you might expect that falling interest rates would cause increased activity in the residential property market: in fact, the market during the '80s and '90s was never more active than when interest rates were at their highest levels.

The idea of cycles is practically synonymous with real estate investment

Personally, I don't know where we are in the cycle, and I'm pretty sure that I don't need to know. I think there is a much simpler factor at work behind fluctuations in property values. And that factor is *affordability*.

WHO CONTROLS THE PRICE OF PROPERTY?

The banks and finance companies indirectly control property prices throughout Australia. How? By controlling the amount that they are prepared to lend on residential property.

And what is that decision based on? Affordability: the borrowers' ability to make the necessary loan repayments, as a percentage of their income.

A typical bank lets people pay 30 - 35% of their disposable income towards mortgage repayments: that's $180 per week of the average wage of $600 per week. This in turn determines the total amount the bank will lend over the life of the loan.

When the market is booming, and banks go beyond these guidelines, weekly repayments increase to the outer limit of *everybody's* comfort zone - and that's when a crash is looming.

Mortgage repayments as a percentage of average weekly earnings

June	Sydney	Melbourne	Brisbane	Adelaide	Perth
	%	%	%	%	%
1980	46.5	28.1	21.8	23.0	25.5
1981	44.9	32.9	25.4	23.2	26.6
1982	45.6	33.4	32.0	25.8	27.4
1983	39.8	29.8	27.9	24.9	25.4
1984	33.6	28.7	24.0	29.6	19.8
1985	35.7	32.6	25.6	31.7	21.3
1986	44.4	42.7	29.3	37.5	27.5
1987	42.3	41.7	28.6	35.1	27.0
1988	44.6	43.2	26.5	29.9	26.5
1989	78.8	56.1	39.7	41.0	45.3
1990	71.4	58.0	43.4	40.6	39.5
1991	53.0	43.8	34.6	33.3	29.3
1992	43.2	33.4	29.5	28.0	25.0
1993	40.1	32.3	27.8	24.9	24.2
1994	39.1	29.4	26.2	22.2	25.1
1995	44.4	31.9	29.3	23.3	28.2
1996	41.8	30.5	26.9	22.2	25.3
1997	36.0	26.6	21.9	18.1	21.1

Source: BIS Shrapnel Pty Ltd

Note that BIS Shrapnel Pty Ltd changed their barometer for measurement from Male Average Weekly Earnings in 1996 to 'Average Weekly Earnings' in 1997 which included full time plus part time total weekly earnings Focus on specifics rather than statistics.

The table opposite shows mortgage repayments as a percentage of male average total weekly earnings since 1980 in the capital cities. You can see that in 1989 and 1990, in Sydney and Melbourne, repayments rose to between 60% and 70% of the average male earnings - and came crashing down, in 1991-2, before settling down to a manageable level again in 1993. And the rise, fall and settling of repayments means the rise, fall and settling of property prices.

If all that looks scary, remember that affordability is quite a simple concept - and you can make it work for you.

AFFORDABILITY ON YOUR SIDE

I recommend building a portfolio of property at the bottom end of the real estate market: that is, within a band where the property is most affordable.

Monitor the value of properties *in relation to male average total weekly earnings:* you can get the statistics from the Australian Bureau of Statistics in the city where you are planning to invest. Establish what you consider an affordable purchase price - around the banks' comfort zone marker of 30-35% - as the *upper limit of what you will pay for an investment property.*

Having an upper limit of 30-35% of average income is consistent with our rental practices as well, since the price of the property will determine the rent we will be able and willing to charge, and we want that to be accessible to 90% of our target market.

Let's see how average property prices compare to our measure of affordability in the capital cities.

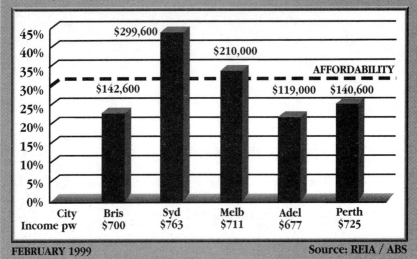

Average property prices

showing mortgage repayments as % of average male weekly earnings

City Income pw	Bris $700	Syd $763	Melb $711	Adel $677	Perth $725
	$142,600	$299,600	$210,000	$119,000	$140,600

AFFORDABILITY

FEBRUARY 1999   Source: REIA / ABS

Brisbane has a reasonable upper end to the affordability range, currently at around 27%. Sydney and Melbourne are, at the moment, pretty close to their peak. Once the price of property in a particular area exceeds the affordability level of the market, it's a good time to stop buying in that area. Historically, the market seems to peak for about two years, after which you can re-enter the market and commence, or continue, building your portfolio.

The point is that affordability is linked to average weekly earnings - and wages and salaries do not, generally, tend to fall. Therefore, at the lower end of the market, there will

Note: For consistency, I have maintained average male weekly earnings rather than BIS Shrapnel barometer.

be less fluctuation in demand, and so in property values. Lower-end property still builds value well - but doesn't lose it badly when the cycle turns.

For example, the following graph shows housing prices in the average residential suburb of Shailer Park, Brisbane, over the past 10 years.

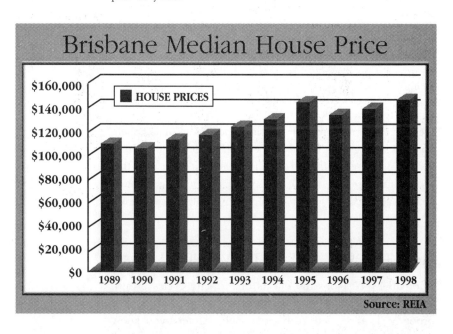

Notice that there was accelerated growth in the years 1988 - 1990 - which fits in with the historic mortgage payment figures listed earlier - but prices seemed to be sheltered from the worst effects of the downturn. You might also be interested to learn that *land* values, in the same area over the same period, showed no downturn at all.

I find that land generally tends to hold its value pretty well: less so, buildings. It's often purchasers' paying over-inflated prices for buildings that causes the mirage referred to as a 'boom'. In my experience, the fall-off in property prices mainly affects the middle to higher range, where investors have paid huge premiums on buildings - inherently shortlived, replaceable products - in the mistaken perception of an under-supply. I saw this most recently in the inner city area of Sydney, in Darling Harbour.

> ## Lower-end property still builds value well - but doesn't lose it badly when the cycle turns.

Over a ten year period, a lot of purchasing mistakes can be recovered and redeemed in housing - but not in units, where you lack the cushion of the land content. You may be sick of my saying it by now, but (one more time): it's the land that offers capital growth; the house is just a vehicle for generating income and tax deductions, in order to offset our outlays on acquiring the land...

THE UPSIDE OF THE BOTTOM END

Affordability cushions the effects of property cycles. It also ensures that, when you decide to sell your investment property (as discussed in the following chapter), you know that anybody with a job will be able to buy it. As you will see from the following table, once a property reaches $250,000 in value, less than 20% of the market can afford to buy it. At about $350,000, your potential buyers are less than 5% of the 'affordable' market.

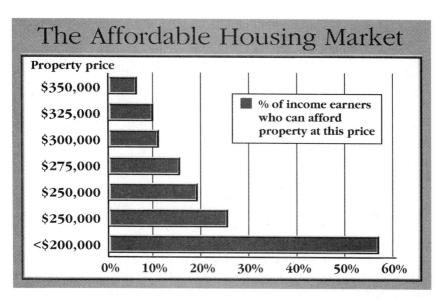

The Affordable Housing Market

Property price

	% of income earners who can afford property at this price
$350,000	
$325,000	
$300,000	
$275,000	
$250,000	
$250,000	
<$200,000	

0%   10%   20%   30%   40%   50%   60%

Notes:

1. Based on average full-time adult weekly income February 1999 - $783.10 (ABS)
2. Assuming 25% deposit, P & I loan @ 7%, 30% gross income apportioned to mortgage payments
3. Approximately 43% of the population earn <$400 per week. They have not been included in the percentages.

So you are better off buying two properties at $150,000 than one property at $300,000. 100% of the qualified market can afford to rent your properties at the price you can afford to charge, thus ensuring that you optimise your income over time - especially since you have your income eggs in more than one basket, spreading the risk of vacancy or other local glitches. And 100% of the qualified market can afford to buy your properties whenever you wish to liquidate your assets.

Case example

One investor from North Queensland had $50,000 to invest. He was considering putting it into one property of around $300,000, which would have shown him an income of $300 per week - with limited depreciation, negative-gearing potential and capital growth. After one of our seminars, in January 1997, he instead bought three new properties for $365,000, borrowing $328,000. The rental income/interest equation left him with no cash outlays, and he got an immediate tax deduction of $18,000 per annum, through depreciation. Most importantly, his properties collectively are now worth over $400,000, and he is using the extra equity to acquire two more properties. Within a short period of time, he will have eight to ten properties in his portfolio, and have dramatically improved his cash position, as a high-bracket tax payer!

(Actually, this man is the Wealth Builder in our case comparison at the end of Chapter 6.)

So, finally, let's look at if, when and how to sell your properties to maximise capital growth.

Chapter 9

Make time work for you

[Step 6]

Some people trade in the property market - constantly buying and selling - quite successfully.

Actually, when I say 'some' people, I mean perhaps 0.01% of investors...

Buying and selling property is *expensive:* around 12% of the initial purchase price can be thrown away in Stamp Duty, fees, charges, commission on re-sale and so on. This is often the forgotten factor when people buy 'fixer uppers'. They add value through renovation and sell on at a higher price - but rarely high enough to offset the costs of renovation *and* the costs of buying and selling!

As you may have noticed, the Wealth Building concept is a longer-term acquisition plan. It's based on long-term factors (like the historical capital growth of residential house-and-land packages, building equity) and offers long-term benefits (sorry, but you don't Get Rich Quick).

The key is to buy, and keep buying, and to *hold.* To let **Assets + Time = Wealth.**

TIME WORKS - WHEN YOU DO!

I might have called this chapter 'Time for Discipline'. A lot of people get excited by the growth history of property, and the prospect of building serious wealth - and often, they lack the discipline, patience and commitment to see it through.

Ironically, this is especially true of some of the high-powered executive types that have come to our seminars. They are happy to agree with all the principles, but confess that building wealth, the way I have portrayed, simply isn't as exciting as going out and doing a deal and making hundreds of thousands of dollars in one 'hit'.

Fair enough. I've got to admit, myself, that our wealth building structure is not all that exciting. It's not a thrill-a-minute gamble. It asks you to wait and 'watch the grass grow'. But there's also a reasonable expectation that beneath that grass - in the land - lie dollars and capital appreciation!

> **Our wealth building structure is not all that exciting.**

Or let's go back to our muscle-building analogy of Chapter 3. The muscle only grows when it is being rested. When muscle-builders become over-enthusiastic, or downright impatient, and do not rest sufficiently after carrying out an exercise, they end up breaking down from stress. Unfortunately, this can occur in the financial situation, too: banks, accountants and advisors are the first ones to point out if your business has grown too quickly or too soon, and to advise you to put the brakes on.

'Making time work for you' is really about establishing the discipline and commitment to acquire six properties over a ten year period, building on the history of the last 90 years, to plan for a 10% per annum capital growth factor.

Let's look again at the basic Financial Goal we introduced in Chapter 3, before all our principles were in place.

Here's where you can end up if you start today, purchasing a property, of the kind we've been talking about, in the way we've been talking about, at an (affordable) $160,000.

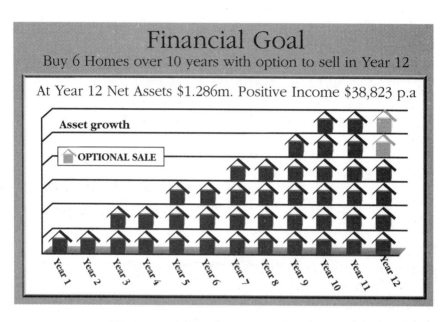

Financial Goal
Buy 6 Homes over 10 years with option to sell in Year 12

At Year 12 Net Assets $1.286m. Positive Income $38,823 p.a

Asset growth

OPTIONAL SALE

Year 1 Year 2 Year 3 Year 4 Year 5 Year 6 Year 7 Year 8 Year 9 Year 10 Year 11 Year 12

OK. Are you sitting down?

If you acquire these properties over a ten year period:
- you will have paid $1,629,000 for your portfolio; and
- you will have a debt of $1,613,000 (if you do not pay off any principal).

Just let that sink in for a moment. It may sound scary. But remember:
- you will also have sufficient *income* to service that entire debt - *and* other outlays.

And here are some more reassuring - perhaps even exciting - numbers.
- In Year 10, your property portfolio will be worth around $2.5 million,
- growing by nearly $250,000 per annum.
- In Year 12, you'll have *net* assets of over $1.4 million,
- *still growing,* at that stage by nearly $300,000 per annum (and rising).

If that doesn't make you feel any happier, let's put those debt numbers into perspective.

- If you started building your six-property portfolio around *1965*, it would have a value today of over a *million dollars*. And even if you had borrowed 100% and never paid a cent of principal, you would have debt of less than *$75,000*.

- If you started building your six-property portfolio around *1975*, the value of your properties would be over a *million dollars* today, and - without your repaying any of the principal - your debt would be around *$220,000*.

- If you started building your six-property portfolio in *1985*, you would still have value of over a *million dollars* today, with a debt (without having repaid principal) of just over *$500,000*.

And you'd also have the rental *income* from the six properties, which would easily service a principal and interest loan *and* give you some income *and* you'd have capital growth of over $100,000 a year, which would *compound* over the next 10 years...

These debts that you might have been carrying from the '60s, '70s or '80s don't seem so scary when you think where you've got to. This may be a helpful perspective for starting your Wealth Building. $1.5 million (in ten years) may seem a lot of debt to carry, but:

- it is being reliably serviced - without drawing on your personal cash flow or other resources; and

- at that stage, your equity is growing by $250,000 - $300,000 per annum.

People often challenge me with the assertion that, since inflation is low, property won't grow at the same rate. Indeed, I read all sorts of 'expert' opinions preaching this as some new financial gospel. Where do they get it from? If you've stayed awake to the property markets in Melbourne and Sydney, for example, during 1996-97, you'd be aware that property tends to rebound to make up for limited capital growth in slower years. We need to look coolly at the effects of inflation. During the '60s, we had an average inflation of approximately 2.5% - and property prices in some capital cities grew at a massive 13% per annum.

My personal opinion is that inflation really just props up building costs, and therefore *units,* which have a high building content. And, throughout the '60s, '70s and '80s, the growth in *house* values, as a percentage, has outperformed units and townhouses.

HOW DO YOU MAKE TIME WORK FOR YOU?

From a long-term perspective, there need be no barriers to wealth building. It merely requires a disciplined commitment in two areas:

1. Keep buying over the ten year period (unless the principle of affordability has been made impossible by a greedy phase of the market in a particular area).

2. Take one step at a time.

We'll look at each of these commitments in turn.

KEEP BUYING

With an average property growth of 10% over the 10 year period, you will have six opportunities to use your increased equity to acquire further property. You might be 'sitting out' of the market for perhaps three years out of the ten.

The time to sit out of the market is when the factors in property pricing (indirectly controlled, as we noted, by the lending institutions) are out of step with average income, and therefore beyond the level of general affordability in a particular area.

The following table was used in Chapter 8 to illustrate the lenders' role in defining affordability. Let's look at it more closely.

Mortgage repayments as a percentage of average weekly earnings					
June	Sydney	Melbourne	Brisbane	Adelaide	Perth
	%	%	%	%	%
1980	46.5	28.1	21.8	23.0	25.5
1981	44.9	32.9	25.4	23.2	26.6
1982	45.6	33.4	32.0	25.8	27.4
1983	39.8	29.8	27.9	24.9	25.4
1984	33.6	28.7	24.0	29.6	19.8
1985	35.7	32.6	25.6	31.7	21.3
1986	44.4	42.7	29.3	37.5	27.5
1987	42.3	41.7	28.6	35.1	27.0
1988	44.6	43.2	26.5	29.9	26.5
1989	78.8	56.1	39.7	41.0	45.3
1990	71.4	58.0	43.4	40.6	39.5
1991	53.0	43.8	34.6	33.3	29.3
1992	43.2	33.4	29.5	28.0	25.0
1993	40.1	32.3	27.8	24.9	24.2
1994	39.1	29.4	26.2	22.2	25.1
1995	44.4	31.9	29.3	23.3	28.2
1996	41.8	30.5	26.9	22.2	25.3
1997	36.0	26.6	21.9	18.1	21.1
				Source: BIS Shrapnel Pty Ltd	

Note that BIS Shrapnel Pty Ltd changed their barometer for measurement from Male Average Weekly Earnings in 1996 to 'Average Weekly Earnings' in 1997 which included full time plus part time total weekly earnings. Focus on specifics rather than statistics.

As we noted before, things went crazy in 1989 and 1990 in Sydney and Melbourne, as repayments went to 60% - 78% of the average male earnings.

House prices crashed in 1991, before settling down in 1992 and 1993. If we were building our portfolio at this time, monitoring the market according to our principle of affordability, we would have sat out of the market in Sydney and Melbourne from 1988 right through to 1991. We could have come back in in 1992, perhaps even picking up prime opportunities because of the desperation of a panicked market, in which the banks are selling up less careful investors. This is called *counter-cyclical buying*. (The moral is: don't be a herd investor. Don't buy when everybody else does, when property begins to rise. Buy when everyone else is selling, and sell when everyone else is buying. Better yet: never sell!)

Don't be a herd investor

Sydney and Melbourne seem particularly vulnerable to boom-time problems, perhaps because of the density and size of their population, and the confidence that the banks derive from having their head offices located in those cities, where they deal with major corporate players. Notice that in Brisbane, Adelaide and Perth, there was no way near the same frenzy of mortgage repayments out of kilter with affordability.

You might have chosen to sit out of the market in Brisbane during 1989/90 - but even if you bought during those times, your capital appreciation still would have shown some growth in 1991-93.

> **Acquiring six properties over a ten year period - and holding onto them as a retirement plan - WORKS.**

In any case, if you use your affordability principles, you can judge when to wait and when to buy again, without over-reaching yourself or slowing your capital growth. And in order to accelerate and maintain your portfolio development, remember: you do need to keep buying.

As we noted in Chapter 7, less than 1.5% of all individual investors acquire more than four properties. With a bit of discipline and commitment to keep buying, you're putting yourself among the very top Wealth Builders.

ONE STEP AT A TIME

Acquiring six properties over a ten year period - and holding onto them as a retirement plan - WORKS.

Of course, you could accelerate or slow down this process, to suit your own capacity and confidence.

The important point is to take each step at a time.

Don't be mesmerised at this stage by the thought of owing $1.5 million, or having to manage six properties. Like climbing a mountain, it may look a long way from the bottom to the top, but you get there one step at a time: one property at a time. Give yourself a year or two to settle in, to work out some of the kinks, to establish your structure firmly, so that there really is no drain on your resources. Let your confidence build with each successful step. And then, when the fresh equity is there, think about purchasing again.

Some people say to me that they just *can't* come to grips with the idea of that amount of debt, or owning six properties: they think, because they can't see themselves, as they are today, going from *here* to *there,* all of a sudden, that it's just not for them. That's like letting the mountain conquer you before you have even taken a step. The thing to remember is that:

- you don't have to do it all at once - just one step at a time; and

- you don't have to do the whole journey with the resources or the perspective that you start with: the journey itself equips you as you go forward.

> Like climbing a mountain, it may look a long way from the bottom to the top, but you get there one step at a time.

'Making time work for you' means trusting that all your resources (equity, knowledge, experience, perspective) will grow and mature as the journey proceeds. You have enough to start with. And, with this structure, *you are in control.* At each step - as at the 'end' of the journey - there are *options,* depending on what you want to achieve and what the market is doing.

Let's look at some of the most attractive of those options.

OPTION 1: CONVERT YOUR LOAN TO PRINCIPAL & INTEREST, AFTER 5 YEARS

I personally like the strategy of converting the investment loan on a property to Principal & Interest, after you have owned that property for five years. Rental income growth of between 3% and 4% per annum should allow you to convert your interest-only loan to P & I in Year 6 or 7 - and *still* maintain a nil cash outlay.

Over time, the tenant will then be paying off your mortgage.

You should be aware that the principal is not tax deductible, so you may, following conversion of the loan, have to pay tax. You should also be aware that in the first five years of a 20-year P & I loan, you only pay off between 12% and 15% of the total principal: it is in the last five years that you really see the compound effect of your principal repayments. However, this is a step in the right direction, and can give you some peace of mind, if you're looking to pay off the principal on multiple properties and hold onto them (as they keep generating income) as a retirement plan and/or to pass on to your kids.

OPTION 2: SELL, AND REPAY YOUR DEBT

Selling one or more of your properties is, of course, an option, in order to reduce some or all of the debt on the rest of your portfolio. You need to think about:

- what to sell and
- when to sell.

Selling is particularly attractive in a boom time, when the market may be more optimistic than realistic.

The best time to sell is when everyone else is buying. And that includes that typical two-year peak in the 'cycle' when affordability parameters seem to have gone out the window! You could see the value of your portfolio increase by 25% - 30% *above* its 'true' value for a two-year period (before coming crashing down). Some investors - and a lot of speculators - try and take advantage of this cyclical movement, which we've learned to identify.

So what happens, if you take advantage of the cyclical peak?

Well, if you sold your *last* two properties (acquired in Years 8 and 10, with the cycle working in your favour), and you sold them in Year 12 at the peak of the market, instead of an average 30% increase, you might have a 50% increase on your purchase price. So, if the properties cost you $550,000 and are now worth $715,000, you may have an opportunity to sell them for $900,000: a profit of $350,000 instead of $165,000.

Capital Gains Tax

When you sell (or otherwise dispose of) an asset acquired after 19th September 1985, you are liable for Capital Gains Tax on any increased value, or profit. In terms of property, your *home* is exempt: investment property, unfortunately, isn't. The amount of taxable capital gain is calculated as the sale price (consideration received) *minus* the acquisition cost of the property, indexed for inflation over the time you've held it. (Don't panic. Most people don't do their own CGT calculations: they simply keep their basic purchase/expenditure/sale records and hand them over to a competent accountant. Highly recommended...)

In our example, Capital Gains Tax is worked out on the $350,000 profit, *less* the CPI (inflation) rate for that period. So if you held those last two properties for two years and four years respectively, and the inflation rate was 4%, the calculation would work as follows.

	Property 5 (Year 8)	Property 6 (Year 10)	Total (Year 12)
Purchase price	$250,000	$300,000	$550,000
Sale Price	$450,000	$450,000	$900,000
Book Profit	$200,000	$150,000	$350,000
Less			
Revised Book Cost (with indexation)	$292,465	$324,480	$616,945
Equals			
Taxable Profit (gain)	$157,535	$125,520	$283,055

You would have to pay Capital Gains Tax on a total of $283,055 (after twelve years of investment). This would amount to $133,000 - based on the *highest* marginal rate of income tax.

Two points to note.

1. Because the allowance for indexation is made each year, the longer you hold the property, the less CGT you will have to pay. However, do sell the *last* two properties you purchased: if you sell the first two, your capital gains will be huge (after all, that's the whole point...).

2. If you've sold during a boom, the property may well have been inflated above its true value by almost the total amount of tax you have to pay! So waiting for the boom glitch in the cycle, and taking that opportunity to sell, is a way of minimising the impact of CGT.

> # Tax is simply a factor of doing business.

Tax is simply a factor of doing business. It's one of the reasons why you might consider *not* selling, but *holding* your properties as they keep generating income over time. If you do choose to sell, you need to be aware that CGT is a factor.

OPTION 3: REDEVELOP THE PROPERTIES WITH A HIGHER-DENSITY ZONING

As we have noted, the population in Australia's major cities is steadily growing.

The solution developed by the Town Planners over the last few years is *urban infill:* that is, the redevelopment of 600 and 700 square metre blocks to accommodate two, three or four dwellings instead of one. This may be an option for you in twenty or thirty years' time, if you are still holding a portfolio (as I recommend). Remember, it's the *land* that's of value.

You won't be able to take advantage of higher density building if you own a town house, or if you share the land with another landlord in a group title, but owning a house does give you this flexibility. In Melbourne, Sydney and Brisbane, they have already allowed dual occupancy, and it won't be long (say, ten to twenty years) before they allow higher density again, on these smaller lots. This may effectively give you the opportunity, with your equity, to build three or four income-generating properties on your allotment. I'd still encourage you not to sell them, but to keep the land for further growth.

This has been the secret of a lot of car yards, which bought fringe CBD sites on main roads, ten to twenty years ago, and now find those sites commanding a premium and being re-developed as fast food restaurants, shopping centres and so on. Even if their businesses have only broken even, these car dealers are very wealthy individuals today, because they owned and held onto the land.

SUMMARY

The benefits of letting time work for you are enormous: just glance back at the Financial Goal graph on page 133.

Perhaps the most important thing I've said in this Chapter, though, is this: TAKE ONE STEP AT A TIME.

If we look too far ahead, before we're confident with where we are and where the next step is, we can scare ourselves with all kinds of mirages of things that might go wrong, that we might not know how to deal with (yet). The thing about mirages is, when you actually get there, they tend to disappear. But confidence is a major part of successful - not stressful - Wealth Building.

So in Part C, I deal with some of the 'What if...?' and 'What about...?' questions that you might still have. I get those questions all the time. And it's great - it's vital - that they get asked. When you're about to start a journey, it's natural to look for potholes in the road. As I said, right at the start, sceptics make the best Wealth Builders. But the fact is, no-one's got a crystal ball. There's no such thing as having 'all the answers' (or even 'all the questions') ahead of time. Sooner or later, you've got to choose to take a first step - and that's when the real answers start coming.

You've just had eight chapters of data, pros and cons, principles and options and suggestions. I'm glad if you feel better informed now than when you started this book. But I'd also like you to keep sight of our starting point: the sense of a journey, and the new possibilities that open up as you dare to think about creating wealth, for yourself and others.

So in Chapter 10, let's look, one more time, at where we're headed.

Chapter 10 [Step 7]

Be all you can be

Early on in this book, I hoped to plant a seed in your mind that, as you begin to build wealth, you may find yourself getting back more than you expected: more than financial rewards. I shared with you my own belief that everything has a purpose - and that, through building wealth, I began to discover mine. I'd always felt I had potential - but for what? I started out with the goal of being wealthy, and it was as I reached that goal that I found the goal posts had moved forever.

How do you feel about the idea of being wealthy? Powerful? Excited? Quietly secure: it's just a way to meet your day-to-day needs and those of your family? Or perhaps a little bit guilty or embarrassed? (Some people do.) What possibilities are you allowing yourself to look forward to? And are they really the best you can expect *for* yourself - and *of* yourself?

One of the qualities shared by wealthy people is that they are pro-active: they see opportunities, and make things happen. You might have glimpsed an opportunity as you read this book. You might even go out and make it happen. And being pro-active tends to make you *more* pro-active, because when you're out there, you begin to notice things that you may not have noticed before, and to have the confidence to do something about them. This kind of mental preparedness may be part of your potential: think how useful it could be in all sorts of areas of your life.

THE BIG PICTURE ON WEALTH

Something like 0.0001% of the world's population controls 99% of the world's wealth.

Apparently, a computer model has demonstrated that if all that wealth was distributed equally amongst every living person, within about fifteen years it would have filtered back to the 0.0001%... Whether this is true or not, isn't it an amazing concept? What it means to me is that those few of us who are fortunate and knowledgeable enough to create, control and enjoy wealth have a responsibility towards those who aren't and don't. We are not just wealthy individuals: we are custodians of the world's wealth in our society.

> **We are not just wealthy individuals: we are custodians of the world's wealth in our society.**

And that means that if you are in the Wealth Building business, you have a purpose and a responsibility *wider* than meeting your own needs and the needs of your family.

"ALL THAT MAN IS, IS INFINITE.
ALL THAT MAN HAS, IS FINITE."

Some people talk as if 'you can't take it with you' is a negative thing, and a reason not to bother creating wealth at all. Personally, I find it an energising and empowering idea. I can't take my wealth with me: therefore, I'll both *enjoy* it - and *pass it on*. While I'm alive, I'm 'minding' a portion of the world's wealth, and I can 'pass it on' in all sorts of ways: in improved living conditions and opportunities for others now, and in self-sustaining capital and wealth-preserving knowledge for the future.

There comes a time in your Wealth Building journey when you realise that you have 'enough' wealth to be able to retire. It became clear to me in 1990 that I was getting close: by 1991, I could have retired with an annual income of $300,000 for the rest of my life. It was what I'd always thought I wanted, but when I got there, retiring on my wealth seemed like a huge cop-out. I still needed a challenge and a purpose. At the same time, I couldn't see making *more* (and more) money, for the sake of it, as very fulfilling or purposeful. And that's when the 'custodian' perspective kicked in, for me.

My wife and I decided to establish our own charitable foundation for homeless youth, the plight of whom had concerned us for some time. As 'luck' (or whatever) would have it, we met husband and wife psychologists Dr Ron and Suwanti Farmer, and together, we established the Toogoolawa Children's Home. We started out in Sydney, providing full-time residential care to youth at risk (generally Wards of the State) who had been psychologically damaged within the family.

TOOGOOLAWA: A PLACE IN THE HEART

The Toogoolawa Children's Home

'Toogoolawa' is an aboriginal word meaning 'a place in the heart': our belief is that, whatever physical abuse children have suffered, there is a place within themselves where they can find healing and strength and meaning.

In the Home's first nine years, we have fostered more than 35 young people - with tremendous success, given that some of them (as young as 11 and 12 years old) had been in anything up to 18 other foster homes before coming to Toogoolawa: many of the kids stay with us until they are 15 or 16 years old and ready to live independently.

In 1993, we moved the home to Brisbane, and since then have expanded Toogoolawa to include a school and community service (initiated by the young people themselves). We now have a residential care programme offering:

- long-term placement for 12-15 year olds
- emergency placement (for periods not longer than 7 days) for 12-15 year olds
- planned respite placement (for periods not longer than 2 weeks) for 12-15 year olds living at home or in other substitute care
- a Shared Family Care Programme, offering long- and short-term placement in caring homes. We recruit, train and supervise foster parents for up to 12 troubled teenagers.

The Toogoolawa School

The school was established in 1998, to offer education and opportunity to kids who have been expelled from, are no longer welcome in, or do not feel fulfilled by, mainstream schooling. When we began to research the need, we were alarmed to find that every year there were up to 300 children aged under 15, in the Brisbane area alone, who had been expelled from the public school system, and weren't attending school.

I don't blame the public school system: these kids are, quite often, 'difficult' and disruptive in a 'normal' classroom environment. But it is their right - and our responsibility - to see they get some type of education. (This is another area where 'expert' opinions and statistics are rampant, and I'm not going to labour the point. But it may interest you to learn that, of the prison population in Australia, 95% are from broken families and over 60% are illiterate. Perhaps, if we start with change in these areas, as a community, we can begin to turn around the social decay that we are all so aware of and so frequently daunted by. Like Wealth Building: start small, and think big. Radical change happens one step at a time.)

> # Radical change happens one step at a time.

The Toogoolawa school offers a basic education and a simple, positive philosophy to live by: that service, truthfulness and consideration for others leads to a happy, fulfilled and effective life. The students are taught not only to read, write and spell, but to speak and listen and calculate - and to strive to discern right from wrong, and to see the value in following the former.

The school also operates as a mobile unit, utilising the ideal learning environment of the outdoors. By combining fun and physical activity with experiential learning techniques, students begin to see learning as immediate and relevant, and develop a sense of responsibility for their choices and actions.

Regular sharing sessions help to develop communication skills - and a sense of community is important too: students are involved in running a soup kitchen and an organic garden, as part of our commitment to community service. We strive for a balance between *support* (with an emphasis on social interaction and exploration of spirituality and ecology) and *challenge,* in order to empower and inspire our students to acknowledge and achieve their potential.

THE SMALL DIFFERENCE
THAT MAKES A BIG DIFFERENCE

In 1994, I was at a dinner sponsored by the Committee for Economic Development of Australia (CEDA), with twelve top business people from major public companies. (In hindsight, I'm not actually sure how I fitted into this group, but it was certainly an eye-opener for all of us.) I was asked to talk about my work with Toogoolawa over the preceding four years, and particularly, about (a) the costs of operating such a charity and (b) how you would measure its performance or 'success'.

I explained that the cost of full-time care and schooling, in the intensive environment we have created, can range from $30,000 - $50,000 per child, per annum. I distinctly recall the comment of one flabbergasted diner, to the effect that such a cost was simply unjustifiable, and that I was wasting my money. Some of the other business people present felt that it was the government's obligation - already sufficiently supported by our taxes - to cater for such needs.

What are we made of?

If you were walking down the street, and you saw, on the other side, an eight-year-old child lying bleeding and crying on the pavement, would you cross the road to help? Of course, there would be plenty of excuses *not* to go... Too busy; late for an appointment (*would* have gone, naturally, but the appointment was very important); new suit, didn't want to get blood on it; the child's out of danger now; anyway, things don't look *that* bad - from where you're standing... The most common excuse for doing nothing is also the most simple: someone else will do it.

And this is exactly what's happening, in effect, in our society, every day. When our psychologist started looking into the incidence of child abuse, we were horrified at the numbers we uncovered - and those were only the cases that had come to the attention of the authorities...

If our children are a reflection of how we are handling our responsibility and moral custodianship, we need to wake up and get our act together - fast.

> The most common excuse for doing nothing is also the most simple: someone else will do it.

At Toogoolawa, we've seen a number of kids who, by the time they are eleven or twelve years old, have been in fifteen foster homes and a dozen schools. After the damage they've sustained - in the supposed 'sanctuary' of their own homes - they don't trust anyone. Their distress bursts out in anger and aggression. And so it begins: they go from home to home and from school to school, setting themselves up for rejection after rejection: the only pattern they've ever known.

But at Toogoolawa, we've seen the vicious circle broken. Some of the kids spend the rest of their adolescence with us. Which means that we can begin to help them work through some of their problems. We can give them time to discover that what has happened to them isn't the best they can expect from other people. And that there is some goodness, after all, in the world - and within themselves. Hence the name Toogoolawa: a place in the heart.

Like Wealth Building, it's a long-term programme: no quick fixes. When kids first come to us, they are - understandably -

pretty angry. Three years later, you can see the anger being channelled into something more positive and supportive for them. They have begun to develop some self esteem, to feel good about themselves, perhaps for the first time in their lives.

SOWING THE SEED...

As you can probably tell, I'm pretty committed to - and excited by - my work with the Toogoolawa project. For the last nine years, I have committed over $220,000 a year to it. And the fact is, it's been *enriching* - perhaps the most fulfilling thing I've done in my life.

I started out only providing the money to run the programme, and assist with the administration: we have a great team of psychologists and social workers who work hands-on with the kids and are a constant inspiration to me and to others who come to take a look at the Toogoolawa effect in action. This soon evolved to me running the school outdoor education and effective communication classes allowing me to share another passion I have for hiking with the kids.

But it's making a small difference that makes a big difference.

We all share the responsibility to maintain humanity and justice and opportunity in our society. My hope is that other businesses could take responsibility and find purpose in funding similar programmes: they have the resources and administrative capabilities that welfare agencies often lack.

As for you, if this is the kind of thing you'd like to get involved in, let me encourage you: it needn't be too far away. Once you have a portfolio of four or five homes, you could use the equity to purchase perhaps an older home, which you could dedicate to people in need. You could still claim it as a negatively-geared tax deduction, and you should still get the benefit of capital growth, despite the building's age.

Why an older home? Well, it depends what you are going to use it for, but we had one great kid at Toogoolawa who used to have a monthly fit of rage and frustration - and put his fist through the wall... (He was with us for three years, and by the end, those rages were down to one every six months. He was responsible for repairing and repainting the wall himself - and he got quite good at it. It was amazing to see the pride he took in patching and painting the plaster, and decorating his room so that the damage - like the anger - didn't have to be a daily part of his life.)

If this is the kind of thing you'd like to get involved in, let me encourage you: it needn't be too far away.

The small difference that makes a big difference...

I'd like to tell you a story, told to me by Dr Ron Farmer.

An old man went down to the beach in the morning, where the surf roared onto the still cool sand at the lowest of the tide. And the beach was covered with starfish, stranded by the tide, as far as the eye could see. And the old man bent and began picking up the starfish and throwing them, one by one, back into the water.

A young runner in a grey tracksuit passed, and stopped, and turned and said: 'What are you doing? Can't you see that you're wasting your time? There are *hundreds* of starfish here. Your throwing a few back won't make a bit of difference.'

The old man simply bent, and picked up another rough shape in his rough hand, and threw the starfish out into the water with a quiet splash. And said: 'It made a difference to that one.'

Finding a wider, deeper purpose for your Wealth Building can enrich you on many levels. It can provide the fire and commitment you need to keep going, to start small and think big: it can positively contribute to your success in building wealth. More importantly, perhaps, it can stretch what you may have seen as the limits of your potential, and what it means to be all you can be.

I call it balancing the material with the spiritual...all is one.

PART C
Any other questions?

Chapter 11
What about...?

This is the chapter where I promised to answer some of the 'Yes But...' and 'What if...?' questions that people often bring to our seminars. I don't want to put doubts in your mind, where none may have existed, but you may find this chapter helpful for added confidence - or perhaps as a prompt to other questions you'll want to ask as you investigate the Wealth Building concept further.

I have arranged the queries in alphabetical order by topic, so you can use this as a quick reference tool, as things occur to you.

ECONOMIC CYCLES

Q: What if property doesn't go up by as much as it has done in the past - or even falls in value?

A: See Chapter 8.

INABILITY TO FIND A TENANT

Q: What if I can't get a tenant for my property?

A: See Chapter 5, and 'Loss of tenant', page 159.

INTEREST RATES

Q: What if interest rates increase?

A: The good news is that when interest rates increase, it means that the economy is moving, and your property is going up in value, and so are rents. The bad news is: your costs are increasing too.

One solution is to lock in your loans: all of them, or a percentage of your portfolio, at any time. Establish with your bank, when you begin your Wealth Building programme, that you'd like to have the flexibility to lock in a rate at any time, or a percentage of your total portfolio loan, given that you may float some as variable and some as fixed. The fixed rate for five years is generally around 1% more than the variable rate. (This may seem a small amount, but you should be looking at each percentage point as costing you $30 - $40 per week in cash going out of your pocket - so you need to watch it very, very closely...)

As I keep saying, don't be greedy. If you are comfortable with your repayments, as they are now, why not lock in?

LOAN PROBLEMS

Q: What if the bank won't lend me the money for a further property on the equity I've got?

A: Basically, either wait - or change banks. Find one which will accept the equity position you want. Make sure you clearly flag your intentions to build a portfolio on this basis. (See Chapter 7.) Don't be suprised if you have to change banks two or three times in your Wealth Building journey. Banks are often more aggressive about winning new business than about keeping 'older' clients...

LOSS OF EMPLOYMENT

Q: What if I lose my job?

A: People on PAYE are often concerned that they may lose their job, and - having built up a portfolio of two, three or four properties - may have to sell in the midst of a downcycle, or worse, while simultaneously losing the income advantages of the 221D PAYE taxation benefits.

OK. Put like that, it sounds pretty bad. But: you can *insure* against losing your job, if it is a realistic concern in your circumstances or area of employment. You might choose to investigate this insurance. However, the simpler option is to 'self insure', by simply slowing down your Wealth Building programme.

It's not a race to acquire six properties. If it takes eight, ten or twelve years, it's not going to make a great deal of difference in the long run. For peace of mind, if you have a job that you feel is not 100% secure, just be a little less aggressive in your expansion programme, for the time being. You may want to have a bit more equity in one property before you acquire the next. Perhaps, rather than starting at 10% equity, start at 20% - 25%. This is not a reason to do *nothing!*

There may be another option. As an employer, I invite my staff to let me know if they are thinking of acquiring an investment property, so that I can give them honest, forward-looking information about their job. Might your employer be amenable to such a discussion?

LOSS OF TENANT

Q: What if my tenants leave suddenly - or damage the property?

A: It's inevitable that you are going to lose a tenant or two over a 10-12 year period. And if you do lose a tenant, it might take you a couple of weeks to clean the place up and find another one. This is just a factor of the rental income business. Get used to the idea - and plan accordingly.

I forecast my income based on 48-49 weeks' rent per year. I also keep a two-week contingency fund in the account for each property - just for incidentals (or 'accidentals').

You can have some assurance. Get a bond from all tenants of at least one month's rent, and require that they pay their rent in advance: preferably monthly, but at least fortnightly. If they're late with their rent, the agent should be on alert to advise you within one or two days, so that arrangements can be made with the tenant, or - if they are having longer-term financial difficulties - so that notices can be given, and the property can be inspected. If tenants wish, they can evade paying rent for up to six weeks, so you might lose up to two week's rent. This is insurable, however.

Assuming that tenants have done *everything* in the Nightmare Tenants' Handbook, they could leave you with a few thousand dollars worth of damage that has to be repaired. *Still* not a reason to panic: this is also insurable, except for your excess, which you can limit to $250. The important thing is, don't wait for the claim: get in and clean the property up as soon as the tenant is evicted. Make sure you get quotes and send them to the insurance company - and *get on with getting your property rented again,* as soon as possible.

In my experience, it comes down to financial management and having that little bit in reserve, tucked away for a rainy day. Losing a bad tenant may seem, for a while, like that rainy day, but (a) it is *not* personal - it happens to all of us; and (b) to be honest, 'good riddance'! It's *not* a good reason to wash your hands of a residential portfolio - or the wealth that comes with it!

RECESSION

See Economic Cycles.

TAX LAW CHANGES

Q: What if the government abolishes negative gearing?

A: In July 1985, the Labour government disallowed the tax benefits of negative gearing. All losses that were generated had to be rolled up into the cost of the property and deducted, at the time the property was sold, from the Capital Gains Tax. Panic!

Well, actually, no. The change to the accounting process wasn't too disastrous for investors at the time, because it *wasn't retrospective:* anyone who owned negatively geared properties prior to 1985 could continue claiming the deductions. More importantly, however, the change in policy caused a *major* stall in investment in the new residential property market. Suddenly, there was a looming (drastic) shortage in the supply of residential housing for a growing rental population, and an economy-dragging downturn in building activity.

The Treasurer was forced to *reintroduce* negative gearing in September 1987. Any residential property investor who purchased properties during the two-year abolition period was allowed to offset their two-year losses against their assessable income for 1987-88. (*Nice* U-turn...)

Negative gearing hit the political agenda again, with the revelation that people had been using the provisions to purchase *shares:* the government was considering re-abolishing negative gearing to close the loophole. But the Prime Minister, John Howard, made a statement at the end of 1997 that: 'Negative gearing would not be abolished on residential property.'

Of course, all we can do is work on the knowledge available to us now, and that is:

- you *can* legitimately negatively gear property;

- the government is unlikely to abolish negative gearing on residential property in the future because of the proven knock-on effects on housing supply and economic activity;

- if the government *did* re-abolish, it wouldn't be done retrospectively, so any purchase that you made today would be within the safety net of today's taxation laws.

It is now more or less inevitable that we will have a goods and services tax of some type, and when the government does introduce a GST, it may review negative gearing and limit it to a total of 120% of the purchase price of a property. (This is to prevent investors borrowing 150% - 200% of the property's value over a period of time, and negatively gearing on that amount.) This would not, in fact, affect our Wealth Building structure at all.

MANAGEMENT HASSLES

Q: Isn't managing one rental property - let alone a whole portfolio - a major hassle?

A: Not necessarily - and *not* if you get someone else to do it for you!

The choice of agent to manage your property is one of the most important you'll make. Often, would-be landlords fall into the trap of going with the agent who offers them the highest rent: this is not necessarily an indicator of ability to manage a property successfully.

The questions to ask of a prospective agent are the same you'd ask of prospective employees. Whom have they worked for before? What references have they got?

In essence, look for agents who (a) have experience in managing a large rent roll; (b) have limited vacancies for any given period of time, and (c) have managed on behalf of landlords for an extensive period of time.

Don't be shy of asking for over half a dozen references (or more!) and make sure you ring them *all*. Include a reference from at least one landlord whose property is vacant at the time: such clients will often give you a clear insight into any agent you are looking to appoint.

The other important point to determine is exactly what the agent is going to do for you, and how much it is going to cost you. Generally, the agent's job will fall into the following categories.

- Furnishing you with a fully-itemised monthly statement

- Conducting full internal and external inspections prior to letting - and every three months, along with photographs of the property and a written report

- Providing direct payment of rent received (within three days of the new month) into the bank account of your choice, or by cheque posted directly to you

- Lodging all bonds with the Bond Board, paying accounts (with your permission and on your behalf) and attending to all leases and notices pertaining to the property

- Liaising with all trades people and inspecting all work prior to payment

- Attending to final inspection on your behalf, prior to the expiry of your 3-month new home maintenance warranty
- Checking all potential tenants' references, prior to consulting with you on their acceptability

Most competent agents will do all of the above for you, and will include it in their management fee.

VALUATIONS

Q: What if the bank refuses to disclose its valuation?

A: This is a *must-have* piece of information. The simple answer is: if one bank won't disclose the valuation to you - find another one that will.

ANY OTHER QUESTIONS?

If you have *any* further 'What about...?' or 'What if...?' (or even 'Where exactly did you get that statistic on...?') questions - GREAT!

Ask a trusted financial or property advisor - or call the Custodian Wealth Builders Group in your state. My colleagues are all fellow Wealth Builders, and can help you answer (or ask) any questions you may have. Sceptics make the best Wealth Builders: we're comfortable with questions. (And answers.)

Contact details follow at the end of the book.

And finally...

Round-up quiz

As promised at the start of the book, here's an opportunity to demonstrate just how much you've learned and remembered of what you've read - and how good you are at looking for answers, once you know what the questions are.

I encourage you to have a go at this quiz now. Let yourself notice how easily the information sorts itself out, and how easily some of the answers come. (You may have to look up one or two: there's an index at the end of the book, if you need help.)

1. In making a Wealth Building investment decision, what would be more important?

   ☐ How you felt about it

   ☐ How it stacked up logically

2. What has shown the higher investment return over the last 10 years?

   ☐ Shares   ☐ Residential property

3. In buying a residential investment property for Wealth Building, what would be more important?

   ☐ Rental returns

   ☐ Taxation benefits

   ☐ Capital growth

4. If you invested in residential property, would you use the same criteria and decision-making process that you used to acquire your own home?

   ☐ Yes   ☐ No

5. Is it prudent for me to acquire property close to where I live?

☐ Yes   ☐ No

6. What would be more important in acquiring an investment property for Wealth Building?

☐ Managing your cash flow

☐ Buying the right property

7. What type of property would show the highest capital growth?

☐ Unit/townhouse

☐ House

☐ Land

8. If you had $50,000 deposit to invest in property, would you be better off buying:

☐ One property for $100,000?

☐ One property for $300,000?

☐ Two properties for $150,000 each?

9. Have a guess at the average house price in your capital city in the following years.

1999 $ _____

1989 $ _____

1979 $ _____

10. Which institution(s) effectively control the affordability of housing in Australia?

☐ Real Estate Institute

☐ Property Developers

☐ Banks

☐ Valuers

11. Is the number of renters of property in Australia:

☐ Increasing?

☐ Decreasing?

12. Approximately what is the PAYE Income Tax on a salary of $45,000?

$ _____

13. Can I use my PAYE tax to build wealth?

☐ Yes   ☐ No

14. What is the maximum percentage you can borrow from a bank (a) on an investment property? and (b) on shares (without a margin call)?

(a) _____ % (b) _____ %

15. Which would be the better of these two properties to purchase for wealth building?

(a) A 'period' home close to the city with 70% land content for $200,000; or

(b) A brand new home 15kms from the city with 50% land content?

Quiz answers

Now check our answers against yours - both in the Start-up Quiz on page 23 and in the Round-up Quiz you've just completed. Give yourself a score out of 14 for each quiz.

1. In making a Wealth Building investment decision, what would be more important?

   ☐ How you felt about it

   ☑ How it stacked up logically

2. What has shown the higher investment return over the last 10 years?

   ☑ Shares

   ☐ Residential property

   NB: In 1997 it was residential property, so this can fluctuate year by year.

3. In buying a residential investment property for Wealth Building, what would be more important?

   ☐ Rental returns

   ☐ Taxation benefits

   ☑ Capital growth

4. If you invested in residential property, would you use the same criteria and decision-making process that you used to acquire your own home?

   ☐ Yes   ☑ No

5. Is it prudent for me to acquire property close to where I live?

☐ Yes ☑ No

6. What would be more important in acquiring an investment property for Wealth Building?

☑ Managing your cash flow

☐ Buying the right property

7. What type of property would show the highest capital growth?

☐ Unit/townhouse

☐ House

☑ Land

8. If you had $50,000 deposit to invest in property, would you be better off buying:

☐ One property for $100,000?

☐ One property for $300,000?

☑ Two properties for $150,000 each?

9. Have a guess at the average house price in your capital city in the following years.

1999 $ _____

1989 $ _____

1979 $ _____   (See page 34)

10. Which institution(s) effectively control the affordability of housing in Australia?

- ☐ Real Estate Institute
- ☐ Property Developers
- ☑ Banks
- ☐ Valuers

11. Is the number of renters of property in Australia:

- ☑ Increasing?
- ☐ Decreasing?

12. Approximately what is the PAYE Income Tax on a salary of $45,000?

<u>$11,952</u>

13. Can I use my PAYE tax to build wealth?

☑ Yes   ☐ No

14. What is the maximum percentage you can borrow from a bank (a) on an investment property? and (b) on shares (without a margin call)?

(a) 90% (b) 50%

15. Which would be the better of these two properties to purchase for wealth building?

(a) A 'period' home close to the city with 70% land content for $200,000; or

(b) A brand new home 15kms from the city with 50% land content?

AND...

Pat yourself on the back. Seriously. Allow yourself to feel good about the knowledge and awareness you've developed. (If you got some 'wrong' answers: great! That's often the best way to learn...)

Especially if the whole property investment 'thing' was new to you, you may have had to take on board a load of unfamiliar terms and information and ideas. So you *know you can*. In fact, I hope you'll be reasonably confident that *you can build wealth*. You can do more - and be more - than perhaps you thought when you started this book.

If you've stayed with me for the whole eleven chapters: thanks. It gives me genuine satisfaction to have shared some of my experience and perspective with you - and to wonder what you might *do* with that information, and those ideas, and your own potential. (Feel free to drop me a line and let me know how you're going. I'd love to know - and will reply.) I hope you will become a fellow Wealth Builder and Custodian. But wherever you go from here:

may you be all you can be.

The Custodian
Wealth Builders
Group

Services offered by the Custodian Wealth Builders Group include:

- Research and market analysis
- Finance
- Wealth Building programmes and workshops
- Property acquisition
- Property management

Contacts:

New South Wales:

Suite 411, Henry Lawson Business Centre

Cary Street, Birkenhead Point, Drummoyne, NSW 2047

Telephone: (02) 9181 1555

Facsimile: (02) 9181 1444

custodian@ozemail.com.au

Victoria

Suite 2, Brighton Business Centre,

3 Male Street, Brighton, VIC 3186

Telephone: (03) 9593 3280

Facsimile: (03) 9593 3285

custwb@ozemail.com.au

Queensland:

PO Box 2256

Nerang MDC 4211

Telephone: (07) 5527 4999

Facsimile: (07) 5527 4955

jlf@onthenet.com.au

Website: www.wealthbuilders.com.au

Custodian Helpline: 1800 174 999

If you have any comments on this book, or would like to let us know how the Wealth Building concept is working for you, you are most welcome to write to John L Fitzgerald at the above address.

If you would like further copies of "Seven Steps to Wealth", please contact the Custodian office nearest you, or post or fax one of the order forms provided at the back of this copy.

CUSTODIAN WealthBuilders

Standing poised in anticipation of challenge
and opportunities,
mind and body in balance,
He summons his talents to realise the
sanctioned visualisation.
With determination, integrity and conviction of truth,
service to humanity is his foundation.
He is honour bound.
"The Custodian"

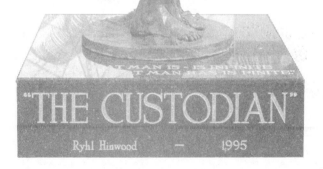

Index

Order form

To: **The Toogoolawa Children's Home Ltd,
PO Box 2256, Nerang MDC, Qld 4211
Fax: (07) 5527 4955**

Name: _____

Address: _____

_____

_____ Postcode: _____

Telephone (for queries only): _____

Please send me the following copies of
'Seven Steps to Wealth' by John L Fitzgerald:

Quantity ____ @ $29.95 each   Subtotal: $ _____

Plus postage & packaging
@ $5.00 per book
(bulk postage rates
available on request)   Subtotal: $ _____
                             Total: $ _____

I enclose a cheque (made payable to The Toogoolawa
Children's Home Ltd) in the amount of $ _____
I hereby authorise you to charge my credit
card (details provided below) in the amount of $ _____

☐ American Express   ☐ Diners Club   ☐ Bankcard

☐ Mastercard   ☐ Visa   Expiry: __ / __

☐☐☐☐ ☐☐☐☐ ☐☐☐☐ ☐☐☐☐

Name as it appears on card (please print):

_____

Authorisation (Signature): _____

Please allow 28 days for delivery